THE
SLAVES' CHAMPION,

OR, A SKETCH OF THE

LIFE, DEEDS, AND HISTORICAL DAYS

OF

WILLIAM WILBERFORCE,

WITH A

PHOTOGRAPHIC PORTRAIT.

WRITTEN

IN COMMEMORATION OF THE CENTENARY OF

HIS BIRTHDAY.

BY THE AUTHOR OF
"THE POPULAR HARMONY OF THE BIBLE," &c. &c.

TO WHICH IS APPENDED
An Account of the Keeping of the Twenty-fifth Birthday of Freedom, &c.

" Such men are not forgot as soon as cold,
Their fragrant memory will outlast their tomb,
Embalm'd for ever in its own perfume."

The Third Edition.

LONDON:
PRINTED FOR THE AUTHOR.
1861.
[The Author of this Work reserves the right of translating it.]

ISBN-13: 978-0-89221-670-3
ISBN-10: 0-89221-670-0

Library of Congress Catalog Number: 2006937539

Printed in the United States of America

For information regarding author interviews, please contact the publicity department at (870) 438-5288.

Please visit our website for other great titles:
www.newleafpress.net

New Leaf Press
A Division of New Leaf Publishing Group

CONTENTS.

Preface.

❈

AUGHT YOU FIND HEREIN,

WORTH KEEPING,

STORE UP.

HONOUR
IS THE SUBJECT OF MY STORY.

Shakspeare.

Thoughts for Old and Young.

"Oh may our thoughts to useful purpose led
Teach us with care the path of life to tread!
Unknown how long to tread that path is given,
Prepared to leave it,—fix our eyes on heaven."

THOUGHT begets thoughts, and the thought that a hundred years ago[1] William Wilberforce, the Slaves' Champion, was born, has suggested the propriety of placing before the reader a few thoughts arising out of that fact, for his consideration, and as a suitable introduction to the following pages, which have been written in Commemoration of the Centenary of his Birth.

Possibly some readers may say "Well, and what of it? There is nothing so extraordinary in the fact that a hundred years have passed."

[1] Wilberforce was born Aug. 24th, 1759: hence, "a hundred years ago" is dated from 1859.

Well, well! the truth is, we don't all see and think the same, and therefore we must bear with each other's infirmities in these, as in other matters—the blind must be legs for the cripple, and he in his turn eyes for the blind; each must help the other, and so jog over the course in brotherly love and with mutual good wishes.

The speaking of a hundred years as having gone for ever, seems as but speaking of a friend who left us but a few days ago; yet how different is the reality from the appearance! How overwhelming the theme which the subject forces upon the attention of a reflecting mind when through the telescope of time he surveys the vast and mighty changes that have taken place in that interval! Our forefathers, who were in the strength of their manhood a hundred years ago, where are they with all they called their own? The millions who inhabited the busy hive of this world a hundred years ago are as if they had not been. A hundred years has obliterated the existence and the very names of tens of millions who were as gay and healthy as probably ourselves are at this day.

The whole race of mankind with some few, very few exceptions, who first saw the light a hundred years ago, have departed, their corruptible parts mingling at this moment with the dust on which they walked, in which they possibly boasted, and from which they were, like ourselves, originally formed. The ravage which a hundred years have inflicted on man and his works is but faintly described and pictured by comparing it to the destruction which an elephant would cause to life and property in treading upon an ant-hill and crushing a colony of busy ants.

Again : what changes have taken place in the past hundred years on the face of nature ! Mere fishing villages have become first and second rate towns ; pleasant fields, the sites of crowded and busy cities; the once silent and meandering rivers have now become the channels for conveying floating hives, filled with men and their labours, to all parts of the world; hills have been bored and levelled; valleys have been filled up, rivers bridged or tunnelled over in order to facilitate communication—giving unity to interest—and by bringing man face to face cementing the bonds of friendship and the holy feelings of common humanity and brotherly love in the bosom of strangers in every land. Nay more, the Old and the New world, and every continent, and almost every important island, have been actually tied together with a rope of iron ; the lightning's properties have been made subservient to transmit our joys and sorrows, our wants and thoughts, to distances unlimited, and with speed second only to that of light itself. There is scarcely a nation upon the earth that has not been brought within almost speaking distance of our own doors, giving unmistakable evidence that the whole world is but *one* great whole for the benefit of *one* great family, in which only *one* interest should predominate and actuate all—the welfare of all.

In the sentence then " a hundred years ago" there is something to see, which it is our interest to be acquainted with; something to learn, which must evince egregious folly to pass unnoticed and unimproved.

It would be easy to dilate upon these subjects, and to give incidents and facts sufficient to fill a hundred folio volumes, but sufficient preliminary observations have been advanced to satisfy the most sceptical that " a hundred years" has within its cycle much on which the mind of every one may reflect and dwell with advantage.

The aged, who have seen with their own eyes the great panorama of life moving before, and in their presence, must recall many and varied recollections —mixed, it may be, with pain and pleasure; the continual change must whisper, as it were, to them that they too must ere long throw off their mortal coil, give place for others, and pass from view; leaving, let it be hoped, a golden ray above the horizon of their setting sun.

To the young, the past hundred years is full of

salutary warnings and warm encouragements; it is replete with instructive examples to guide and influence them in their journey through life, that, when dying, they also may leave behind them evidence that every day of their life was, in consequence of the bright examples before them, a page in which the history of their own usefulness was recorded for the instruction and benefit of others. To them, also, the past century must declare most distinctly that the *now* is theirs; that the *past* was their pilot, and that the *future* shall tell of the use they have made of their advantages; that posterity shall either cast bright and glorious beams amid the recollection of all that is associated with their memory, or consign their having once existed to oblivion and dark forgetfulness; that posterity shall either regard their existence in the light of a blessing, or designate them as only worthless encumberers of the earth—useless posts in the road to improvements; a blank in the laws of creation; a something called *man*, born for no use, living for no purpose, a drone in the hive, a machine which, for want of use, rusted itself to nonentity.

To every one at all able and willing to think, the subject which "a hundred years ago" suggests, must promote proper feelings within them; it must conduce to benefit the thinker, give action to sound and matured resolutions, and nerve the will to strive, under the blessing of God, honestly, heartily, and cheerfully to carry out the design the Creator had in placing them in the station in which each may find himself located.

Again: who can call to mind, or read of the scenes which have been continually shifting, immerging, emerging, and dissolving, without being forcibly impressed with the strongest convictions that the life of man is short and evanescent; that his strongest and apparently most enduring works are mutable, and, withal, that the world is only his workshop, in which, as an apprentice, he is fitting himself for higher and nobler employment, where all is immutability, established and embellished with the glorious presence of Divinity itself.

That the hundred years gone by has been a period in which evil and good have been actively combating for their respective claims, must be evident to the most superficial of readers; but to persons interested in the good of their fellow-men, the combat has been regarded with more than ordinary interest; many an eye of faith has looked forward to, and silent prayers moved, that victory might be won, however costly the sacrifice, for the ultimate happiness of the whole human family.

In the political world, during this period, how many dynasties have changed masters, and thrones been annihilated! What horrors have been enacted, and how much blood has been spilt to second the ambitious designs and maintain the wills of tyrants and oppressors! What convulsions have perplexed and harassed the religious world in this cycle! What daring assaults have been made on " the faith once delivered to the saints," by those who say " There is no God," as well as by those who, while they believe, live as if they neither cared for nor feared one! What heinous crimes, and how much secret wickedness, have been committed during the light of day and the darkness of night, which have occurred so many times in a century!

But, to change the picture—What good has been done, and how far may she claim victory on her side? Those heavenward-pointing spires, the glory and embellishment of our native scenery, which by thousands raise their tongueless voice, tell their own tale of good achieved : they are the monuments of the victories Christianity and freedom have won for man's eternal welfare. The presence of foreigners among us, from every land, tells that civilization has advanced, and is winning her cause. The presence of men, whose faces wear all shades of colour, gives incontestable proof that Freedom has broken her bonds, having shaken slavery from off her shoulders, and is again mounting her rightful seat in the great family circle of nations, from which she had been so long excluded. The

numerous schools, the multitude of private and public
asylums and charitable institutions; reading-rooms,
museums, learned societies, manufactories, and
printing-offices; the legion of cheap and sound pub-
lications; the millions and tens of millions of copies
of that precious word, which "giveth life and understanding," that have been circulated throughout the
world,—each and all of these bear testimony, and
answer the question most emphatically, declaring
that in the past hundred years more good has been
done than in any preceding century, and that greater
advancement has been made in all that can make a
man or a people " healthy, wealthy, and wise,"—wise
and happy here, rich and happy hereafter,—than
was ever made by any nation before. What need
for deep feelings of gratitude, and remembering the
injunction, "Take heed lest ye fall!"

While the short-comings and disadvantages which
overshadowed and hid many of the virtues possessed
by our forefathers are so open to our censure, their
state to some extent is our own; and while the recollection thereof reminds us that we require
something more within, than the custom of the
world offers, and the law of nature teaches, to make
us truly great, and humanize our feelings and actions
above the maxim, " An eye for an eye, and a tooth
for a tooth," our present blessings speak in voices
louder than thunder, that we are responsible creatures,

bound by the law of the light within us, by the law of humanity, by the law of civilization, by the law of that light which the knowledge of Christ has vouchsafed to dispense, and by the law of the God who made us, to leave behind us blessings and examples, which our children may receive and embrace for their own welfare, and improve for the happiness of their successors—bequeathing to them the sweet savour of having been useful in our day and generation, they, in their turn, may transmit the perfume thereof, improved and strengthened, and so be known to posterity as the instruments by which a stationary or retrograde state of society was prevented, its progressive prosperity accelerated and adorned, and its attractiveness made so magnetic, as to draw all within its power, and make each partake of its invaluable properties.   Of each such benefactor it shall then be said :—

"Unborn generations shall live to bless thee."

Such are some few of the reflections which must of necessity occur to, and possess, a regulated and well-disposed mind, when contemplating the mighty revolution which everything, in connection with man, has experienced in the period of a century—a revolution which has changed the face of nature, no less than the character, condition, and habits of man, and even extended itself to the very language of his mother tongue.

Before quitting these remarks, let us take the opportunity to correct one or two popular errors, which it is feared have had no little baneful influence on the minds and actions of some, and been the means of inculcating misconceptions respecting individual responsibilities and individual duties.

I am not an old man, but I hesitate not to say, that I have heard scores and scores of times, persons to whom one would give the credit of knowing better, excuse with all seriousness, their apathy, lukewarmness, and carelessness, by, "Oh! what does it matter? it will be all the same a hundred years hence." Now, it has often struck me that such persons did not actually know the meaning of what they said, and only gave vent to the over-pressure of an idle constitution, by letting off some of its useless vapour by a safety-valve, over which they evidently appeared to have no control,—the key having, as I conjecture, been mislaid or lost in their youth. If any of my readers have entertained the same or similar delusive proverbs, let them be assured (and I only echo the opinion of the wise), that they cherish an enemy in their bosoms. That it will not be all the same we know; we know, from personal observation, that it is not the same now as it was twenty-five years ago; and our children will, moreover, learn by experience, and especially if they neglect now the educational advantages within their reach, that it

will not be the same twenty-five years hence. The
sun may shine, and the clouds shade the earth; all
the functions of nature and the laws of the universe
may, and probably will, a thousand years hence,
perform as regularly the duties originally assigned to
them by their Creator thousands of years ago, as
they do at the present time; but the state of the
inhabitants of the world, the character of society,
and all appertaining to and emanating from man,
will not be the same; his habits, his feelings, his
wants, and his whole design, are not stationary—the
world a hundred years hence must be either better
or worse than it is at this day. And this truism
becomes more impressive when we feel that much of
the moulding thereof depends upon us, individually
and collectively; that to us belongs the responsible
and glorious task of making it better, and that our
acts and lives now must either be productive of
future good, or future evil, to generations succeeding
us. To each the poet says:—

> " A nation's tastes depend on you,
> Perhaps a nation's virtue too."

Knowing this, is there, I would earnestly ask, an
individual so devoid of every manly feeling as to
shun the task of endeavouring to benefit the world
by his good example? I trust not. If we possess
one iota of pride and moral courage within our
breasts; if we have one spark of true patriotism

alive within us — one drop of the essence of Christianity; and, to use a common but expressive phrase, if the John-Bullism of which we talk, and the British stamina of which we boast so much, mean anything and be of any worth, then it must most undoubtedly warm our hearts, and cause us to make the welfare of our fellow-creatures the one sole object of our lives, and the mainspring of all our actions.

This leads us to expose the fallaciousness contained in the other popular error, viz:—"The good men do in their lives dies with them; but their evil deeds are engraved in adamant and brass." This is as monstrously untrue as the assertions contained in the former proverb. That there are persons who do acts of charity, and the like, that they may have praise of men, cannot be denied; and that there are even some who do evil that they may be applauded by, and appear great in the eyes of, their associates —the worthless—is equally true; but to conceive an individual possessed of the attributes of even common decency, neglecting to do good, and committing evil that he may have his name engraved on tablets and perpetuated by monuments, (for such are the impressions the proverb suggests), is so preposterous, so utterly at variance to what a sane person expects, so thoroughly inimical to our better and finer feelings, that, in charity, we hope not one single case could be cited where the maxim had wholly taken so lamentable a direction in the mind. To do good for the sake of praise is selfishness in the superlative degree; to forget the good conferred is base ingratitude; to do evil for the sake of fame is most impious, and to perpetuate evil, most vile.

Thank God, it is not the custom in this or any other civilized country, to applaud evil deeds, much less to record them in brass; if remembered at all, it is with pain, and simply for the sake of the warning their recollection carries with it. On the other hand, the good that men do for the sake of doing good, does not die with them. It may not, and it is not necessary, that it should in every instance be recorded in brass, or known to the world from pole to pole. If it is not known, and its influence felt at every inhabited spot on which the sun of heaven shines, it has its own little world, in which it stands forth as a pillar of light; it has its own peculiar tablets, more valuable than gold or the finest marble, on which it is engraved—it is written on the hearts and impressed imperishably on the memories of the lovers of good; and like a precious heirloom, handed down from father to son, till often the act only remains, the name of the doer having long ceased to be coupled with it. Moreover, if we are Christians indeed, and have faith, even so small as a grain of mustard seed, we know, and believe,

14

that the good done here, if it be done because God first loved us, does not die with the doer, but is recorded to all eternity in Heaven.

If, then, these errors are errors indeed, what an impetus must the knowledge that it will *not* be all the same a hundred years hence, and that the good that one does, does *not* die with them, give to all our actions! It has influenced the conduct of the wisest and best of men; thousands there have been, and still are, noble and illustrious too, who have devoted and still are devoting the whole of their energies disinterestedly for the temporal and eternal welfare of their species — men there are, who are still treading the earth with us, who are contented to forget their own conveniencies and comforts in their anxieties and solicitude for the good of their fellow-men — many, who though rich and noble, yet deign to become servants in the cause of humanity. Away then with these "popular" errors, these deceiving proverbs, and if witnesses be necessary to give these delusions the lie, let there be produced, among other examples, the living sparks which are burning brightly within the breasts of millions, at the present moment, for the memory of Wilberforce and the lasting good which he effected, and with which his name is associated. Rest assured that—

"Such men are not forgot as soon as cold,
Their fragrant memory will outlast their tomb,
Embalm'd for ever in its own perfume."

Having spoken in the preceding remarks of the good that noble and illustrious, individuals are disseminating around them, it leads us to observe that the privilege and opportunity of doing good, and benefiting our species, are not confined wholly to those blessed with affluence and taking rank among the great ones of the earth—Wilberforce himself was a middle-class man—it extends to all classes and conditions of men—the peer and the peasant, the rich and the poor. Real greatness does not depend upon one's standing in, but the good he spreads among, society. A useful man, whatever and wherever his station, must be a great man and a blessing to those around him; an idle and cold-hearted one, on the contrary, is, let him be rich or poor, not only a useless individual, but a veritable curse to all among whom he may unfortunately be thrown. Neither the gilded coach, the well-filled purse, nor the delicate hand, necessarily confers the title great on the possessor thereof; nor does the thread-worn coat, the empty purse, nor the corn-palmed hand, deprive the owner of such, to his title to it.

It matters not where the lot of either may be cast; it may be at the plough-tail in the one instance, and in the other, in the council chamber of his sovereign—true nobility and true greatness may show, and has shown, itself at both stations.

Thousands of instances are recorded of persons moving in the highest ranks of society, adding by their actions nobleness to nobility, and greatness to eminence; and among the middle and lower classes, of persons who have not only been the architects of their own fortune, but by their usefulness the creators of their own nobility and greatness. May each of my younger readers consider this, and if either of them has the laudable ambition to aspire to such true nobility and greatness, let me say unto such in the words of One who went about doing good, "Go and do thou likewise."

Go, act in the present—the future is treacherously uncertain—to-morrow belongs not to you—the good of *one* day may produce lasting blessing and perhaps immortal fame to the doer. Every day has its good to be done and its evil to be avoided. Put it not off "till a more convenient season," for

> "Our lives are like rivers gliding free,
> To that unfathom'd boundless sea,
> The silent grave:"—

where works of love, of faith, and hope, can work no more. The day is not far distant—we know not how near — when it shall be said of us, in the sublime language of inspiration, "The silver cord" has been "loosed; the golden bowl broken; the pitcher broken at the fountain; the wheel broken at the cistern; the dust to return to the earth as it

was, and the spirit to return unto God who gave it."
Then

> "Act—act in the living present!
> Heart within, and God o'er head."

By so doing, you will not only ensure to yourself
that satisfaction which gives peace and contentment
to the mind when looking back upon a well-spent
life, but you will, should God bless you with gray
hairs, reap for your old age and memory that tribute
of crowning praise contained in the saying, " he
walked with God, and was useful to, and in the
favour of, man." A purse is useless to him who has
no money to put into it; and so is the life of that
man whose actions are not governed by those high
principles which true religion, under the grace of
God, can give him abundantly. Ganganelli, the
Italian, was right, when he told his friend, that
" Man, in order to be wise and happy, should begin
betimes to look upon God as the origin and end of
all things;" and that "reason and faith should, at
the same time, teach him that, by observing neither
worship nor the laws, he abases himself to the condition of brutes." He who acts contrary to this
teaching—this doing everything as in the sight of,
and for the honour of, God—is anything but a great
man, and had better not act at all. And bear in
mind that neither the building of pyramids, nor the
founding of kingdoms, can give that greatness I

am desirous of impressing upon the notice of my
readers—the greatness I wish my young friends to
aim at, consists in benefiting their species, while
living a consistent and Christian life themselves.
The world may call such greatness weak-mindedness;
but be not daunted at its cowardice and sneers—it
is a greatness your Heavenly Master has directed
you to strive to attain, by the example of His own
life. Thanks be to God we have numerous examples
for our encouragement. Therefore with a good
heart, and "God o'er head," may the

> "Lives of great men all remind us
> We can make our lives sublime,
> And, departing, leave behind us,
> Foot-prints on the sands of Time."

Living Thoughts.

"Who that bears
A human bosom, hath not often felt
How dear are all those ties which bind our race
In gentleness together."

WHETHER in his day he was a great philosopher, poet, musician, or statesman, the centenary of the birth of an eminent man, always presents a fitting opportunity for his successors to look back into the interval which has passed since he was ushered into being: it affords a pleasing task to scan the career of such a one, and to pick out those favourable salient points in his life, which have combined to entitle his name and memory to be made the red-letter-day in a nation's recollection and esteem. But if this be so pleasing an employment when having reference to eminence in general, how much more pleasing and gratifying does it become when eminence in station, or learning, or science, is adorned

with Christian virtues, with greatness and goodness
of heart—when philanthropy and piety give lustre
to the character, and greatness to the individual
whose name and memory we thus delight to honour
and cherish! These additional qualifications do, by
a single touch, as it were, transform polished silver
into the brightest and purest gold; they give, as it
were, the master-touch to the portrait which before
only bore a faint semblance to perfection.

A desire to probe into and peruse the personal
incidents and collateral events which entertwined,
made up, and surrounded the life and times of one
so regarded, is so inherent and congenial to the
noble feelings of Englishmen, and persons in
general, that it begets within them somewhat of that
reverence which possessed the minds of the ancients,
and caused them to deify and worship the saviours
of their country and the benefactors of the people.
The recollection of his usefulness kindles within the
bosom of the true patriot, the warmest emotions of
esteem : in his life, everything which surrounded
him is made, by the fondest wish, to partake of the
essence of his greatness—to the mind of the well-
wisher of his country, the smallest act of one, whom
he regards as having, while living, been a benefactor
to his fellow-men, an ornament to society, and an
honour to his country, is justly viewed as a blessing,
and the means of adding an additional and lasting

ray of glory on the land that gave him birth. Indeed, he is regarded as something more than an ordinary being, and, consequently, the "keeping" of his centenary birthday is looked forward to, by every one of his admirers, with as much implanted earnest fondness, and with no less anticipated delight than that which, in our own childhood, we anticipated the joys of each returning natal day. His death is forgotten in the recollection of the fact that he once lived, to be a blessing; the mind forgets for the instant that he is not among the living, and fondly makes his admirer believe that he will, in the company of others, gather around the venerable centenarian on his natal day, to present him with chaplets of evergreens, and sentiments of affection. The mind would willingly obliterate, "He being dead," in the esteem it entertains, and the conviction forced upon it, that he "yet speaketh," and is seen living in his acts still among the people.

These are some of the laudable feelings which gratitude will awaken in the bosom of all sensible persons, which, when properly carried out, frequently give rise to those Public Commemorations which it is a pleasure to see so willingly and heartily cele· brated in honour of acknowledged worth. It is a pleasure, because, to the living, it does this good,— while honouring the departed, it tells to the world that gratitude is alive among us; it tells to the rising generation that it is only for them (any one of them) to do that which is worthy of merit in their lives, and when they are dead it will live in the memory and affection of their posterity. There needs, let it be remembered, no excuse for showing acts of gratitude for such merit—gratitude was never yet called to an account, or required to write an apology, for her feelings; and never will she leave, let us hope, the territory of the heart of a true-born son of Old England. Gratitude is a gift from Heaven quite as much as bread; and he is a madman who spurns either from him, and refuses to be benefited by them. Think of this, young readers, and cherish gratitude in your hearts, and by your lives show that you lay the same burden on others.

Now, it is well known, that it is not every spider that spins a web, catches a fly ere he is destroyed; so neither is it, let it be recollected, every worker in the world's workshop who lives to be benefited by his labours—the industry of both may be admired long after the workers have perished; but such is the law of nature and the will of their Creator. Similarly, perhaps, may the inscrutable reasons and the veiled expediency be accounted for, which is so tacitly adhered to by England in tardily evincing, in some instances, her appreciation of, and her willingness to reward, the labours and merits of her *living* sons. Still, as if to show them that they must live by faith in the promises of rewards in things temporal as well as things spiritual, there never was a nation so ready and so keenly alive to the policy and justice of honouring the ashes and keeping alive the memory of her departed great: nay, often rewarding the merits, earned by the father, upon his children for successive generations. It matters little what our individual political opinions be, or the diversities in sentiments of creed entertained, the peer and the peasant, the rich and the poor, the learned and the unlearned, are all and each ready to revere the memory of the worthy dead, and with heart and soul, purse and hands, if needs be, to aid in weaving the laurel *in memoriam* to the truly good and great of those who have shed their light, while living, to benefit the human race, and left a luminous galaxy, when departing, to guide and cheer those who may live after them in finding the paths of freedom, happiness, and honour. It does not follow that stony registers must perpetuate the fame of such : it is enough to know that one's

" own goodness
Shall live, when earthly monument is none."

It is the innate birthright of Britons to regard the deeds of their forefathers with more than ordinary or commonplace interest—whether they consist of acts of noble valour by sea or land, or be shown as honourable footprints impressed by perseverance in the arts or the sciences; or distinction attained in the Cabinet, or the study; in the Church or at the Bar, or in the truly noble cause of philanthropy—they are recalled with pleasure, gratify the sensibility of, and make a lasting impression on, the finer traits of the human character—pride in the chivalrous and valorous acts, the indomitable perseverance, and nobleness of character shown in their ancestors, and act as strong inducements for the present generation to follow their praiseworthy examples: the remembrance of them nerves against cowardice, idleness, and selfishness, and stirs their posterity to see that such glorious testimonies of nobleness of ancestral pride be not tarnished or veiled by the contrary acts of those to whom they are transmitted. "Keepsake, sir?" said one in reply to a question, "yes, I have one: my father's name, his deeds, and his love to God and man, which I will keep and, on my dying bed, hand with my last blessing to my children, uneclipsed by any black spot in my own life: I will hand it to them framed with my own deeds and piety, which shall be no disfigurement to the blessed souvenir." How beautiful is this greatness, and how exalted the nobility which is seen in the truly chivalrous father! When such truly noble British pride as this, in conjunction with that preceding, ceases to be part and parcel of the existence of the true-born Briton, then shall the land that gave him birth be blotted out of the map of nations, and its organic structure hide itself in shame below the briny billows which now lave her shore, and every wave which shall then roll over it, shall chant curses on the memory of those unworthy ones whose baseness caused them to leave their original bounds. But this can never be so long as Britain is true to her original pride—so long as the blood of Britain's fathers flows in the manly veins of her children. England has been, and shall remain, an eminent example to all the world of the pride she has in the name of her worthy sons, and the scrupulous jealousy with which she sees that their merits are handed down untarnished to posterity. England says to every one of her sons, respecting their worthy predecessors, their

> . . . . "worthinisse
> Remaines recorded in so many hearts,
> As time nor malice cannot wrong your right
> To th' inheritance of;"—

and to her sons now living and may yet be born,

> . . . . . "Fame you must possesse—
> You, that have built, by your great deserts,
> Out of small meanes, a farre more exquisit
> And glorious dwelling for your honoured name
> Than all the gold that leaden minds can frame."

Yes, "fame" and honour too; for such shall be firmly built in the memory of their nation!

But if there be any one human qualification

which calls for special recognition above others, it is that essence of greatness which Christianity has so strongly enjoined upon her disciples—brotherly love —a spirit of philanthropy — philanthropy which manifests itself in not only maintaining the unity of the human species and striving to remove the barrier which prejudice, narrow views, and selfishness have set up in opposition to common sense, common justice, and disinterestedness, but which goes further, shows itself by "*treating*," as Humboldt says, "*all* mankind without reference to religion, nation, or colour, as one fraternity—one great community,"—fitted for the highest objects destined for it by its Creator, and strives as its ultimate object to let all, whether bond or free, find their freedom in the knowledge that the religion of Christ can make them free indeed. Common humanity is one of the noblest leading principles in the history of mankind, but when it has so high a motive as this, it then becomes not only the exponent of the finest part of our humanity, but the positive proof that we have been with Jesus ourselves, and are desirous to seek our fellow that we may say to him, "We have found Jesus—come and see," so that many Nathanaels (whatever the colour of their skin (may be induced to come and exclaim, "Rabbi, thou art the Son of God, thou art the king of Israel."

Philanthropy has a noble origin, and a rightful throne in every heart, for God made the heart, Christ washed out the dust which the whirlwind of sin had drifted into it, and the Holy Spirit relighted and regarnished it with flames and mirrors of love : the Three in One then took their seat in it, but, and let it never be forgotten, reserved one seat vacant— one for our brother. He, then, who allows his brother to occupy that seat in his heart, makes him a part of himself, and at once becomes a true philanthropist, and as such makes the temporal and spiritual welfare of the new occupant the ruling principle of his life. This humanity, this ruling principle, was the foundation of Christianity, was promulgated by the Christian religion, and by the influence of the same religion it has been kept alive, and, like leaven, is gradually permeating the whole body of the human race—its oxydating power, if I may use the word in this sense, is silently and surely eating its way through the manacles of the slave, and destroying the power of the sword—it is bringing freedom and ensuring peace ; in other words, establishing love and dethroning that inhumanity which

" Makes countless thousands mourn."

And hear ye this, ye cruel slave-owners—proslavery men and journals—" Whosoever doeth not righteousness [justice] is not of God, neither he that loveth not his brother." If you drive your brother (black or white) out of your heart, you may depend that the Divine seat is vacated also.

Moreover, bear in mind that the vacant seat is universal, as well as free. I care not who he may be, I fearlessly assert, he is not worthy of the name of *man* if he allows that seat to be only partially occupied—occupied by the white man only — the negro must be there as well—and if the negro and the oppressed be there, then that heart will not find rest till they be free—free as that heart itself is—free as God made man free before free man took freedom, most tyrannically, from free man. He will endeavour to secure to his black brother even more than that liberty which Cowper has so beautifully pictured :

> "There is yet a liberty, unsung
> By poets, and by senators unpraised,
> Which monarchs cannot grant, nor all the powers
> Of earth and hell confederate take away :
> A liberty, which persecution, fraud,
> Oppression, prisons, have no power to bind:
> Which whoso tastes can be enslaved no more.
> 'Tis liberty of heart derived from Heaven,
> Bought with His blood, who gave it to mankind,
> And sealed it with the same token."

God said, "In the sweat of thy brow shalt thou eat bread," but nowhere that one man shall be a slave—a beast of burden to another. It is true God "made man upright," and that he has "sought out many inventions," but the most impious, the most unrighteous, the most hell-born of all his inventions is that of slavery—a traffic in human flesh.

If, my readers, your house were entered by thieves, your property taken, your wives, children, and relatives, treated with violence before your eyes, and in the sight of bystanders, would you not resist? Would you not with your own arm, and call upon those who stood by to help you? You would, and more, if those who saw and knew of the violence and would not aid, but coolly regarded it as no affair of theirs, you would stigmatize them as most inhuman, most cruel, and as not a shade before the thieves themselves—you would regard them as abettors and accessors of the acts. Such then is the view you must take of the diabolical treatment to which the slave and the negro are subjected. You do, my readers, know of the tyranny and cruelty to which the negro is daily subjected, and if, therefore, you do not with every nerve you possess come to his help, you are not a jot before the trafficker in human flesh—if not the principal to, you are accessory both before and after, the cruelty and oppression under which the poor negro, your brother, is daily suffering and dying. Let, therefore, your love for him constrain you to give him a seat in your heart, and so show your brotherly and manly feelings.

It has been said that a Queen of England once declared that the name of a certain town which she had lost would, after her death, be found engraven upon her heart. Speaking by comparison, one would be led to foretell that if a trafficker in human flesh were opened after he was dead, either no heart would be found, or one so black, that it would not be known from the colour of the poor negro's skin, for whom, while living, it had no feeling. And what shall we say of the heart of the free man, who cares little or nothing for the wrongs and cruelties which his enslaved black brother suffers? Why, just this, my readers, — he has a heart of stone, blood of frozen ice, a soul not larger than a bodkin's point, and is totally unworthy of the freedom he enjoys. Oh! then, enlarge your soul, let your heart of flesh beat, your blood warm, and your whole energies be devoted to the crying cause of the negro. Abel's blood called not more loudly to heaven for vengeance than the heart-rending sufferings of the negro do even now for your intercession and humanity on his behalf. If you have humanity, if you have the spirit of Christianity, he will not cry in vain. You will give him that seat in your heart, and love him as Christ loved you.

In writing thus for the cause of the negro, I do not forget the true axiom—"Look at home first," neither would I ignore the rights of the white man.

I know where it is said—" If any provide not for
his own, especially for those of his own house, he
hath denied the faith, and is worse than an infidel."
But I feel that we do not do enough for the poor
negro, and might do more for the slaves of home if
we would.

Nothing can more beautifully express and more
forcibly set forth the true principle which actuates
and shows the genuine philanthropist, and one possessed of those brotherly and manly feelings, than
the words of the poet Wither :—

> "No outward marke we have to know,
>   Who thine, oh Christ, may be,
> Vntill a Christian loue doth show,
>   Who appertains to thee :
> For knowledge may be reach'd vnto,
>   And formal Iustice gain'd ;
> But till each other loue we doe
>   Both Faith and Workes are faign'd."

This is universal love—love for the enslaved as well
as for the free. When, therefore, we discover greatness stamped with the die of such love, and of so
elastic and ductile a character that it is seen extending itself like so many radiating circles from
home and fatherland to the tens of millions in
distant realms, the possessor of such is not only a
philanthropist indeed, but a hero in every sense of
the word ; all the laudations and civic crowns of old
Rome could not more decidedly emblazon and pro-

claim it; it speaks its own merits, and paints its honours silently but indelibly on every good man's heart—and that is worth far more than all the triumphal crowns and pyramidical monuments that the whole world could offer.

Well, then, one who deserved all such honours, and was even more than the hero—who was a Christian soldier as well as a philanthropist — dwelt among us only a few years, scarcely a quarter of a century ago, and in memory of whom these pages were written. Scarcely a quarter of a century ago, his merits were recognized in the honour which the nation paid to his mortal remains; but a greater honour is demanded for him, and such as he, in the living thoughts of posterity: they must be recorded in the heart as the glorious and most emphatic evidences of our never-dying affection and gratitude for our ever-to-be-remembered countryman and benefactor. I say *our* benefactor, for the negro is *our* brother and one of the great human family. His life and heroic deeds must and will ever deserve a place in the memory of the thoughtful. Thoughts of such heroes as Wilberforce, Clarkson, Stephen, Zachary Macaulay, and Joseph Sturge, must be living thoughts of gratitude, and ever worthy examples for encouragement and imitation : no bare cold thoughts like those which possess us in our daily routine, they must be warm and elastic, I had

almost said angelic—for while we think of them
here we may cast our eyes for their abode

> Where angels sing and dwell.

Sweet is the fragrance of such men's deeds to the
memory, and precious the balm of consolation
which the recollection of them silently conveys to
the soul in times when she is constrained to paint
to herself the horrors inflicted on our race by the
rough and jagged angles which appear so often on
the human character: it tells her that man's nature
is not so bad and inhuman as some would make it
to be; that the human heart only wants the living
spark, and it is then all on fire of love for its
brother; the blacker his skin, and the heavier that
brother's bondage, the more intensely will the fire
burn to set him free.

It has been asserted that " on the opinion of men
depends our fame "—[not of *one* man, although his
opinion may be given in the shape of a leader or
article in the journals—still it is only the opinion of
one, viz., the writer of the article.]   If this be true,
the philanthropist can never be forgotten ; all hold
him in the highest esteem ; he is above all in the
living thoughts of the memory ; honour for him
cannot be too frequently manifested, nor his deeds
too often recited, to gratify the desire, and give opportunity for praise.   Of others the world may proclaim,

> " Be thou as chaste as ice, as pure as snow,
> Thou shalt not escape calumny."

But of the philanthropist, in his character as such, the sum of the "Black Word" for him is "He was born, not for himself, therefore we will speak tenderly of his feelings—he was born to love and serve all mankind." His love for his universal brother has kept from him that which taints the acts and motives of not a few—so-called benefactors of mankind—selfishness.

If there be one among the thousands of philanthropists to whom the "living thought" is due, it is "the venerable patriarch in the cause of slaves," as Lord Brougham so graphically called William Wilberforce, the instrument by which no fewer than 800,000 slaves were set free—felt that their bodies, souls, and all that belong to them, they might no longer say belonged to "massa wid de whip," but to God and themselves. He and his cause will live through all times; yea, when slavery in every part of the world shall be only known as an historic and long-gone-by fact which once blotted the map of the free-born community, the name and deeds of Wilberforce and his compeers will live and be as dear to the recollection as they are at this day—they cannot die—they will be among the Living Thoughts of England's worthy sons long after those of Tasso, Petrarch, Milton—and I had almost said our immortal Shakespeare—are forgotten. More : it shall be said, when even the great works and eminent men of the present day are lost in oblivion, chaos, and regarded as myths, that,

> " To sire from grandsire, and from sire to son,
> Throughout their generations, did pursue,
> With purpose, and hereditary love,
> Most steadfast and unwavering"

to remember the name of William Wilberforce and his love for his white and black brothers.

With an hereditary love not less steadfast, and with a feeling of reverence for the name of Wilberforce, (whose " works of faith, and labours of love," are, we doubt not, now crowned with " an exceeding great reward " with those happy spirits who " through faith and patience, inherit the promises"), let us give him a hallowed place in our Living Thoughts, and in the Sketch of his Life and Times endeavour to gather many thoughts and instances of example for our consideration, admiration, and profit. And here I would affectionately admonish my younger readers to use discretion in the gathering, inasmuch as they will have men and actions surrounding the Life of Wilberforce, which, if they should (and I see little reason why they should not) take an interest in, and read particulars for themselves, they will find *outwardly appear* to be quite as valuable as any examples which his life may offer for their imitation. The outside may, and they will find often does, appear ripe and golden ;

but within they will discover only maggots and worthless refuse. "All is not gold that glitters," remember; and while it is our interest and duty carefully to choose the purer metal, it is no less our duty most scrupulously to reject the base alloy, however temptingly it may be offered to satisfy our wants and desires. "St." Bernard has this so much to the purpose, that I am sure my young readers will not scold me for bringing his saying to their notice. Latin scholars may translate for themselves, but for others a translation is affixed :—*Si quid mali vides in alio, vide si in te est; si est, rejice, si non est, abstine. Si quid boni vides in alio, vide si in te est; si est, retine, si non est, assume.*

> "If any evil thou canst see
>   In other men to dwell,
> Reject it soon, if 'tis in thee;
>   If not, it still repel.
> If any good have other men,
>   See if thou hast it too;
> If so, retain it fast; but then,
>   If not, pray get it, do."

The Slaves' Champion.

"Such men are raised to station and command,
When Providence means mercy to a land;
He speaks, and they appear, to Him they owe
Skill to direct, and strength to strike the blow."

UNLIKE many of his worthy coadjutors, both dead and living, who *privately* laboured with that silent eloquence of a good life and sincerity of purpose, which fortified their cause, and enabled them to be instrumental in bringing about that glorious harvest of Abolition and Slave Emancipation of which hundreds of thousands are at this present hour enjoying the fruit, the subject of our memoir was a *public* man— one whose private and public life not only stand out in the boldest characters as an honourable member of the British senate, but as a truly Christian patriot, and one whose name to all ages will be regarded as having been the watchword of negro freedom, while his deeds will be looked upon as conferring upon his nation the greatest honour that any nation can desire and be proud of—giving to man his "birthright:" freedom to the slave. While every good man, to whom the silent labours of those departed are known, will drop a tear of affection and gratitude over their graves, and lift up his daily orisons of gratitude to Heaven for the blessing of having had them sent among us, not only for our betterment, but to aid in giving rights to the wronged; he will, with the same aspiration, breathe his heartfelt thankfulness to "the Giver of all good," that many of their fellow-helpers are still spared, not only to receive our warmest sentiments of love and gratitude, and to bear their testimony, before the rising generation, to the zeal and greatness of heart which characterized the Slaves' Champions, but to tell to the civilized world that the benevolent work of *universal* freedom did not stop with the clarion voice of Wilberforce and the death of his compeers, but is still steadily and satisfactorily progressing to that all-to-be-desired time when slavery shall be known no more. While, I say, this feeling must possess our bosoms for the departed friends of freedom, and the living champions in the same cause, the name and deeds of Wilberforce demand all the honour that individual and public gratitude can evince for his memory, or that can be conveyed to the public through those channels which, next to the blessing of freedom itself, are dear to old England, viz., through the medium of an unfettered voice and an unfettered press.

Surrounded by great actors in the world's drama, and taking a prominent part in many of the scenes which passed during a most eventful period in the history of this country, the name of William Wilberforce stands prominently forward as dear to the recollection of many living, who knew him personally, appreciated his Christian character, the sincerity of all his acts, his spotless honour, the energies he devoted to the cause of humanity, and to all those objects he considered likely to conduce to the moral improvement of mankind; to all, his name is associated with feelings of profound reverence as, in the words of Lord Brougham, "The venerable patriarch of the cause of slaves." By all, therefore, who value freedom and the memory of a good man, the following Sketch of his Life, and Times, in Commemoration of the Centenary of his Birth will be read, it is presumed, with that interest which the life of a Christian patriot is sure to command from every kindred breast, and lover of the benefactors of our species.

As an instructive aid to fixing the chronology of the biography of Wilberforce in the minds of youth (for whom this work is more especially written), I shall make frequent reference to contemporaneous events, and the political history of his times, feeling sure, from experience, that such a plan is always attended with benefit to the youthful readers of memoirs of great men.

While yet the English nation was recovering from the horrors which the tragedy connected with the Black Hole at Calcutta had inflicted on its nerves, and the sound-wave of victory which arose from Plassy had scarcely died from the ears of our foes east and west of that plain; while the gallantry and daring sagacity of Clive in the East, was laying the foundation for a hundred years of commercial advantages to ourselves, the blessings of freedom to the conquered Hindoo and Mahometan people, and opening a way for the introduction of the saving doctrine of Christianity—that one sole religion on which national greatness or individual freedom can find a secure basis and permanent existence—while the strong hand of Pitt was holding the helm of the nation, and his master-spirit was guiding the tossed and straining barque of the British constitution through the troubled waters of a universal war, and steering her past the rocks and quicksands of Home and Foreign policy and intrigues; while the popular indignation manifested at the loss of Minorca, and the fierce clamour which sent the unfortunate Byng to a premature and martyr's grave, had scarcely cooled down; while the gallant Wolfe was climbing the heights of Quebec, which was to be at one and the same moment the road to his victory over the French and his own death; ensuring thereby the conquest of Canada to his nation, and immortal fame in the memory of his people to all posterity; while on the outskirts of civilization, where the vices of polished and savage life were exercising a baneful influence on the policy of Europe, the knife of the assassin was being prepared to take the life of an autocrat sovereign; while the preaching of White-field was drawing thousands to his views at home, and the poetry of Metastasio was electrifying Southern Europe; while the ink was flowing from the pens of Goldsmith, Sterne, and Gray, and infidelity was being promulgated by Rosseau and Voltaire; while Hunter was following up his surgical labours, and Cook was preparing for his future circumnavigation of the globe: both to confer lasting benefits on the human race;—about the time these things were taking place, the town which was the first to shut its gates against Charles I. gave cradle to the subject of our memoir—to that one who, in after life, was to stand in the Senate-house of the British nation, and there lift his voice, successfully, against oppression, tyranny, and slavery, and on behalf of freedom, common humanity, and brotherly love; one, who should show to the world his utter abhorrence and the illegality of Flesh-Money, as the staunch old burghers of Hull did to the forces of Charles their antipathy to monopolies, the Court of High Commissioners, the Star Chamber, and the illegality of Ship-money—one, who should be the champion of that despised race of whom this time a hundred years ago, and for years after, it might be said :—

> ———— " Spurn'd, degraded, trampled, and oppress'd,
> The negro-exile languish'd in the West,
> With nothing left of life but hated breath,
> And not a hope, except the hope in death!"

Such were some of the most important events and the state of society which a century ago immediately preceded and ushered in the nativity of William Wilberforce, on the 24th of August, 1759—a day also possessing an unenviable reputation as being the anniversary of the horrid massacre of 70,000 Huguenots or French Protestants, throughout the kingdom of France, attended with circumstances of the most shocking treachery and cruelty—it began at Paris in the night of the festival of St. Bartholomew, August 24th, 1572, by secret orders from Charles IX., King of France, at the instigation, it is said, of his mother the Queen-dowager, Catherine de Medicis. I mention this coincidence, because it is worthy of being remembered. Wilberforce's birthday, which might be said to sound the trumpet of life and freedom to 800,000 human beings, proclaimed at midnight, two centuries before, the iron hand of death and oppression to more than 70,000 of our fellow-creatures. The slaves in the West, and the poor Huguenots of France, were not, before the emancipation of the former, very dissimilar in the treatment they received; and the characters of the masters to whom they were morally bound were equally true parallels. Of both classes of victims it may be justly said—

——— " Their moans
The vales redoubled to the hills, and they
To heaven."

But, to return to the subject of our memoir—On, as before observed, the 24th of August, 1759 (the same year in which William Pitt, on the 28th of May, first saw the light), William Wilberforce was born at Hull, in a house in High Street, and was baptized in Trinity Church in the following month. He was descended from an ancient family, originally settled at Wilberfoss, near Pocklington, in the county of York; whence was derived the family name; the manor which had been possessed by his ancestors, was alienated by W. Wilberfoss, who sold it in 1719. The ancient orthography of this local designation was changed to Wilberforce by the members of a branch of the family which flourished in the city of York in the seventeenth century. The Slaves' Champion was the son of Robert Wilberforce, of Kingston-upon-Hull; and his grandfather had twice held the office of mayor

in that borough: indeed, his ancestors had been, it
seems, for many years successfully engaged in trade
in that town. We may here observe, that some of
his forefathers were connected with the *Thorntons*,
and hence the intimacy between William Wilberforce
and that family: an intimacy which a similarity of
excellence, humanity, and piety, served to bind in
the strongest bond of union.

The young philanthropist, we are told, was a feeble,
delicate child, but was blessed with a vigorous mind
and an affectionate temper; so critical was the state
of his health in early years, that in after-life, he was
wont to congratulate himself that he was not born in
less civilized days, when it would have been thought
impossible to rear so tender a child. However,
without entering into all the minutiæ of his infantine
and juvenile days, we may reasonably suppose that
little Wilberforce was cherished with all that affection
which springs from the bosom of fond parents, and
that he passed through all those interesting and
progressive steps common to the little masculine
olive-branches of the present day; the pap and cradle;
the pleasing toy and the A B C; top, marbles, and
the Latin Grammar, no doubt had their respective
weight upon the budding years of the future British
senator.

The death of his father occurring when he was nine
years old, the care of his education devolved on his

mother. At this period he was transferred to the guardianship of a pious uncle and aunt, residing at Wimbledon, near London, under whose roof new examples and powerful influences soon showed their effects in his youthful life. His aunt was an admirer of Whitefield. Not only did the pious aunt's influence manifest itself in all the letters which her warm-hearted nephew wrote—and which then, as all through his life, bespoke the dictates of an ingenuous mind—but while under her roof, the interesting child was often made the subject of the earnest and affectionate prayers of the venerable John Newton, to whom he was introduced by his pious relatives. We can easily imagine that one so beloved, and so admired, by his fond aunt and her friends, as young Wilberforce unquestionably was, would frequently become the object of those kind comments which often in spite of the dictates of common sense, will urge the tongue to give utterance to that which the heart would most fondly hope is justly due to their prodigy; we can fancy the kind aunt repeating, with almost paternal feelings, some such inward sentiments of joy, hope, and resignation, as those which the charming lines of Moultrie so beautifully depict:—

> "His presence is like sunshine
>   Sent to gladden home and hearth,
> To comfort us in all our griefs,
>   And sweeten all our mirth;

> Should he grow up to riper years,
>   God grant his heart may prove
> As sweet a home for heavenly grace
>   As now for earthly love ;
> And if beside his grave the tears
>   Our aching eyes must dim,
> God comfort us for all the love
>   That we shall lose in him."

But over the abode of cheerful piety at Wimbledon, was soon to spread a cloud to bring many sad and sorrowful regrets—the warm-hearted boy was to be removed to a less religious atmosphere. His letters had betrayed the fact that his mind was imbued with religion, and this seems to have alarmed his relatives and friends at Hull, for his mother repaired with all despatch to London, for the express purpose of removing him from the dangerous contagion, as they deemed his aunt's principles, and from that which they believed would be detrimental to his future well-being, and imperil his friendship with those of his Yorkshire acquaintance. All that could tend to quench and obliterate his pious feelings was had recourse to with more than common solicitude and zealous infatuation by his friends (?) at Hull. The ball-room, cards, and the theatre, were all tried by turns, to draw his mind from religion, and to beget within him a love of the world and its pleasures; but all failed for a time to have their intended effect; he resisted their gaudy tinsel, and when first taken to the theatre, he says,

" it was almost by force." By degrees, however, the world captured the young soldier, and he gradually acquired a relish for the new and jovial life into which he had been forced. What a lesson this! And if it were not with the hope that it may be of service to parents and the friends of youth in the present day, my pen should not be the means of refreshing the mind on such past sad examples as those set before young Wilberforce. His relations now living will therefore, I trust, kindly view the repetition of them in this light, and exonerate me from any intention of speaking lightly and unbecomingly of the dead. Wilberforce himself says, " As grandson of one of the principal inhabitants" (of Hull), " I was everywhere invited and caressed: my voice and my love of music, made me still more acceptable. The religious impressions which I had gained at Wimbledon, continued for a considerable time after my return to Hull, but my friends spared no pains to stifle them. I may almost say, no pious parents ever laboured more to impress a beloved child with sentiments of piety, than they did to give me a taste for the world and its diversions." But "God moves in a mysterious way," and notwithstanding the fact that up to the latter end of the year 1785, there was not an inch of ground in his heart but what the world might call its own, the early impressions which he received at Wimbledon were not to be totally lost; the pious seed sown by his aunt, and the fruit which it ultimately produced, most beautifully illustrate the divine maxim, " Cast thy bread upon the waters, and thou shalt find it after many days." Of the gratifying change in his life we shall speak more particularly hereafter; let us therefore return with young Wilberforce and his mother to Hull.

Having been some time at the Free School at Pocklington, he was subsequently placed under the tuition of the Rev. Joseph Milner, a clergyman distinguished by his writings; but particularly as being the author of that ecclesiastical work known as a *History of the Church of Christ,* and which, to the present day, holds a prominent place in the estimation of Christians in general. The preaching of this divine appears to have made some impressions on his youthful mind, but to what extent it is not now possible to determine; possibly the germ of many of those peculiar religious opinions, which in after-life he repeatedly advocated from the press, may have been received while under that excellent man's tuition. While we leave the embryo M.P. at the feet of his tutor, and to the examples of his friends (from the time he left Wimbledon till that at which he took up his abode at College), we will look outside and see what had been, and was still, going on during that interval.

We have already learnt from his own words, how much of his outer life was made up—passed while Blackstone was labouring at his *Commentaries*, and England's great luminary, Sam. Johnson, was weekly plodding to the "Turk's Head" Literary Club, receiving complimentary honours from Universities and Royalty—including pen-and-ink blows of irritation from Macpherson; while Garrick was treading the boards of Old Drury, and reaching the summit of excellence as an actor; while John Howard (a true philanthropist) was silently wending his way from dungeon to dungeon in the ardent and unremitting exercises of Christian Charity; while Walpole (the benign, but non-patron of artists and men of letters) was busy with the printing press at Strawberry Hill, and poor Chatterton was dying of starvation; while Bishop Lowth was on the episcopal throne, now occupied by William Wilberforce's energetic and Christian son; while the partition of Poland, and the revolution in Sweden, were engaging the attention of political circles, and the suppression of the Jesuits by Pope Clement XIV. was astonishing the Church and Cabinets of the Continent; while Kennicot was labouring over biblical and oriental lore, and Buffon was engaged in the field of natural history; while the tutor of young Chesterfield had not yet written that fatal name which, in the year 1777, brought him to the

scaffold; while Wilkes was an outlaw, and the
terror of a " General Warrant" was filling the hearts
of the innocent with fear; while Edmund Burke
was delivering his maiden speech in the House of
Commons, and Sheridan was gaining the highest
reputation at Covent Garden, and preparing his
voice to deliver that triumphal oratorical eloquence
on behalf of India, impeaching Warren Hastings,
and which Lord Byron has celebrated in the
following lines :—

> " When the loud cry of trampled Hindostan
> Arose to Heav'n in her appeal to man,
> His was the thunder, his the avenging rod,
> The wrath—the delegated voice of God!
> Which shook the nations through his lips, and blazed,
> Till vanquished senates trembled as they praised."

And further—while Spain refused to explain or
modify that " Family Compact" which caused us to
declare war against her, and forced her to exclaim,
" Peace with England, and war with all the world ;"
while Bute and Pitt were at hammer-and-tongs
respecting the advantages and disadvantages which
had accrued by that treaty which had given to us
the American territory; again, while, for the first
time in the annals of England, seats in Parliament became matters of bargain and sale, and the
Sovereign sought to establish his throne at the
expense of a venal Commons and an unpopular
nobility; while internal quarrels, riots, destitution,

and failures in manufacturing districts, set all parties by the ears; throwing a portion of the taxes of this country on our American colonies, gave rise to angry feelings abroad, and led them to take up arms against us; while Lord Chatham was forfeiting the confidence of the people by wearing the state livery of an earldom, and losing the power of that oratory he once possessed; while the tables were turning in his favour, and he and his hostile train were driving the Duke of Grafton from power, and lifting Lord North into his place; while even this last nobleman's acts were rousing the ire of the indignant Chatham and causing him to give vent to expressions, for the too free use of which he was likely to be called unpleasantly to an account; while the Lord Mayor of London was lecturing his Sovereign at home, and acts of violence were bringing the King's troops into collision with the American colonists abroad, and the great Chatham was drawing towards the close of his life—while all these outward struggles had been harassing the nation, young Wilberforce had been preparing himself to enter, as a student, the College of St. John's at Cambridge. Finally, at the very time that Wilberforce was packing up in Hull to start for the University, and probably in the act of receiving the warm good wishes and parting shake of the hand from his friends, the news of the Battle of Bunker's Hill, and the Declaration of Independence by the United States of America, was being wafted across the Atlantic for the information and to the chagrin of the British nation.

Whether the subject of our memoir was or was not interested in any of these national matters, is of little importance: one thing is certain, that the great actors in the great drama going on in the outer world cared little for him, and he in his turn was quite unconcerned touching the definition the burly and testy Lexicographer chose to give to the word "oats" in his famous lexicon; his own little world no doubt had its own sun and clouds, which alternately gladdened and shaded his daily trials. He might have felt and repeated, when his little world did not go so smoothly as he could wish, what older heads have had cause to feel was their position at such moments—that the world is

> "A stage, where every man must play a part,
> And mine, a *sad* one."

There were more senses than one in which the early life of Wilberforce may be called a *sad* one; but perhaps the saddest was that which deprived him of an early and continued Christian and properly disciplined training, and the loss of which he himself regretted to the close of his life.

It was about 1775 that he entered as a student at St. John's, where he took the degree of Bachelor of Arts in 1781, and that of Master of Arts in 1788.

At College he contracted an intimacy with William Pitt, and with Isaac Milner (the younger brother of Joseph Milner), who afterwards became Dean of Carlisle.

In his eighteenth year, by the death of his grandfather, and also his uncle at Wimbledon, he inherited an independent property under the sole guardianship of his mother, and at once became "lord of himself," so that the very first night that he arrived at Cambridge, he was introduced, to use his own words, to "as licentious a set of men as can well be conceived. They drank hard, and their conversation was even worse than their lives." What a contrast between the young philanthropist's introduction to his aunt's villa at Wimbledon, and that he now received as a "freshman" at Alma Mater! Worldly-minded and thoughtless as he was, he was amazed and horror-struck at the low character and vicious life of his new companions; but though he rowed too often in the same boat, and too frequently entered into many of the scenes in which his gay associates found pleasure, he never sunk so low as to allow himself to be dragged into the corroding mire of their vile excesses: just the fringe of formal religion made up his inner life, and all outside of that was idle amusements—card parties—and a round of gaiety which just stopped where excess began. It is not necessary to follow him into all those pleasures into which he eagerly ran, and to drag out from the grave of time the errors into which his foolish companions and the buoyancy and elastic spirit of his youth led him; but we may just sum up the contrast in saying, that the Bible which was known to him at Wimbledon, and the songs of Zion which at that picture of a pious English home were sung, were now, at Cambridge, the one a shunned and unopened volume, and the other supplanted by the cup and song of Bacchanalian mirth and riotings. Who would have recognized in the same person the nephew sitting at the feet of his aunt, hearing the words which belonged to his eternal peace, and the student in the rooms of his profane companions at Cambridge, his ears being there defiled by all that was obscene, and his soul poisoned and put in jeopardy of eternal ruin! The time which was thus so injuriously and unprofitably consumed, and the evil examples which he here so readily imbibed, he himself declares he could not look back upon in after-life "without unfeigned remorse," and with shame, that he had sacrificed so much on the shrine of pleasure, folly, and sin, in his growing years. Thank God that we, who live now, know that he was not an immolated victim on that shrine, although his pious friends of that day, feared that his life would only produce tares with scarcely a grain of wheat. I say we have reason to thank

God, and millions have a like reason to bless Providence, that although the good seed which was sown early at Wimbledon was thickly covered with tares and weeds, the latter died after a terrible struggle for possession, and the former burst forth with luxuriance, and with fruit most abundantly and most profitably.

> " Truth is always strange,
> Stranger than fiction."

Let us not judge; let us not entertain feelings partaking of too hypercritical a tincture; manhood and boyhood always see with different eyes; we are too prone to forget the follies of our own youth in the storm of *debris* which rolled around and covered many of the brighter spots in the life of the youthful years of those we are apt to criticise. Let him that was without sin and folly in his youth cast the first injurious slur on the memory of the youthful Wilberforce.

On attaining his majority, he frequently took up his residence at the beautiful villa at Wimbledon. Many were the charms which that villa possessed,— and oh! that he had continued to drink of that draught which he had tasted there ten or twelve years before. While standing on that hallowed ground, did ever his soul look around, and the thoughts of the past constrain him to cry out, " Oh! that one would give me to drink of the water of the well from which my aunt drew for me, living waters." What his feelings were when he stood there not only a man, but the owner of that very villa, where so many happy days had been spent, must be a matter of conjecture. Here, however, we must leave him till the circumstances of which we shall speak in the next section, brought him before the world in the character of a public man. No doubt he realized many of those feelings which most of us remember as being contained in the poem of the "Old Oaken Bucket," when he revisited his youthful haunts :—

"How dear to my heart are the scenes of my childhood,
  When fond recollection recalls them to view!
  The orchard, the meadow, and deep tangled wild wood,
  And every loved spot which my infancy knew," &c.

Wilberforce the Senator.

---✦✕✦---

"It seems but yesterday
I was a child: to-morrow to be grey."

THE breath of the great Lord Chatham had scarcely ceased hovering around the walls of the Senate House in which it had so often, while living, been heard to echo and re-echo the dictates of his master-spirit; about the time that Henry (now Lord) Brougham—our present illustrious and venerable example of industry, learning, and humanity—was an infant, kicking and squalling, in his cradle; about the time that the cannon of Gibraltar was opening its destructive fire on the besiegers of that fortress, and while the Gordon riots were disturbing the peaceable inhabitants of London, and death was removing the Empress Maria Theresa from a world of sorrow, the student of St. John's was stepping from the abode of Learning to the platform on which Themis reigns supreme—from Cambridge to a seat in the British Senate.

On his coming of age, just before the general election of 1780, he was returned as a member of Parliament, amidst much popular triumph, for his native town, Kingston-upon Hull. New dangers now surrounded him and threatened to bring about his ruin. He entered freely into all the life of London "fast" men; became a member of various clubs; was courted by the gay and noble, gambled and played, followed all the allurements of vice, and indulged in every pleasure that could stamp him as a man of the world; and, most extraordinary, though flattered by Royalty, almost worshipped by fashionable circles, and mixing in all sorts of vanity, he neither debased himself, by forfeiting his independence, nor finally lost his moral purity. The observation that was made in reference to the providential care, and which was manifested in the life of another, is peculiarly applicable to that of Wilberforce at this time :—" A hand was preserving him from the wreck of ruin, which he neither knew nor saw."

I shall here quote the words of one of his numerous biographers as fitly showing his position at this juncture : " In a season of intense political excitement in 1783, he took part in the discussion of affairs in a great county meeting at York. The weather was cold and stormy; the castle-yard was crowded; and men of powerful frames and strong lungs could scarcely make themselves heard, when up rose a small feeble man, with a shrill but musical voice. The multitude were arrested and enchained by his eloquence for more than an hour; and before his speech was finished, the acclamations of the freeholders burst forth, 'We will have this man for our county member.' This was his own heart's ambition. But so bold was the idea, and so improbable its realization, that he concealed it in his own breast, till the feeling of the county rendered his election certain. In after years, he saw in this event something more than gratified ambition. It was one of ' the notables of his life,' which he recorded in his journal thirty years after in these terms:—' My being raised to my present situation just before I became acquainted with the truth, and one year and a half before I in any degree experienced its power— this, humanly speaking, would not have taken place afterwards." The commanding position which he acquired as member for Yorkshire, sustained by an eloquence worthy of it, was an important element in the influence which, at a later period, he brought to bear on the abolition of the slave trade, and many of those improvements which he advocated and saw carried out.

In February, 1783, he advocated the treaty of peace concluded with the United States and their allies, during the short-lived Administration, when Lord Shelburne (the Marquis of Lansdowne) presided over the Treasury, and Mr. Pitt, with whom Wilberforce had connected himself by the closest and most intimate friendship, was Chancellor of the Exchequer. On this occasion he seconded the motion for an address of thanks to his Majesty, observing that at that moment tranquillity was essentially requisite for the country after " a mad and calamitous war." While the wisdom of Franklin and the genius of Washington had thus defeated the obstinacy and the insane stupidity of *our* George, the merits and clear-headedness of *their* George, on the other side of the Atlantic, gained for him the honour of being their first President at this period ; and while Sir Joshua Reynolds was sitting before his easel, and the great Mozart was dotting those staves which should for all ages thrill and inspire the soul with heavenly strains, our own legislative assembly was being prorogued, to give rest to the shaking brain of majesty, and an opportunity for members to " enjoy the races," &c., and which Wilberforce did, he says himself, to the fullest extent, and with a heart bent on all its vanities.

Having gone down to York on the prorogation of the House, he there, in 1784, " spent his twenty-fifth birth-day at the top wave and highest flow of all those frivolous amusements which had swallowed up so large a portion of his youth." In conjunction with some of his college friends, he proposed to make a tour on the Continent. Being disappointed by the refusal of a friend, at York, whom he invited to join him, he, most fortunately, asked Isaac Milner (afterwards Dean of Carlisle,) who consented to accompany him. Here, let us take notice, commenced to ooze that stream which was to drive back, ere long, the dark and powerful wave which had for so many years borne him on towards the whirlpool of destruction. At this time his companions were all "jolly fellows well met;" but ere many months were to pass, the veil was to be withdrawn, and their eyes open to their danger. Hear what Wilberforce himself says of his companion. "Though Milner's religious principles were, even now (1784-5), much the same as in later life, yet they had at this time little practical effect on his conduct. He was free from every taint of vice, but not more attentive than others to religion. He appeared in all respects like an ordinary man of the world, mixing, like myself, in all companies, and joining, as readily as others, in the prevalent Sunday parties. Indeed, when I engaged him as my companion in my tour, I knew not that he had any deeper principles. The first time I discovered it, was at the public table at Scarborough. The conversation turned on Mr. Stillingfleet (Rector of Hotham), and I spoke of him as a good man, but one who carried things too far. 'Not a bit too far,' said Milner; and to this opinion he adhered when we renewed the conversation in the evening on the sands. This declaration greatly surprised me; and it was agreed that at some future time we would talk the matter over. Had I known at first what his opinions were, it would have decided me against making the offer; so true is it that a gracious hand leads us in ways that we know not, and blesses us not only without, but even against our plans and inclinations." [And Mr. Wilberforce might have added, that it is generally those persons who care least about religion, who are loudest in their cry that the pious in matters of religion " carry things too far."] However, a lodgment was made in his conscience, and matter for serious thinking suggested, which left him no peace till he had discovered that he had not carried religious matters far enough for his own safety. At Nice he and his friend Milner often discussed religion in a kind of speculative manner; but neither felt the power of their conversation—the one cold and lukewarm, and the other gay, and counting the whole of his blessing to consist in the enjoyment of the things and pleasures of this world, and the society of his mother, sister, and two female friends, who were his companions in the tour. He was

> The diamond—yet unpolished,
> Whose hidden light was clouded; the gem—
> Whose value no merchant could prize—
> A Peruvian mine unopened.

But duty called him from the retreat where he had been luxuriating with his friends. He and Milner were on the point of leaving: the former to resume his parliamentary duties, when, accidentally, a copy of Doddridge's *Rise and Progress* fell into his hands; casting his eyes hastily over its pages, he asked Milner's opinion of it. "It is one of the best books ever written: let us take it with us, and read on our journey," was the reply of Milner. They did: and it led him to determine, at some future time, to examine the Scriptures for himself, to see if things were stated there in the same manner. Naturally of a weakly constitution, his health seemed to give way; many were the dangers which beset his personal safety; but neither of these things appeared to make the least impression on his mind. At Wimbledon gathered the gay and the thoughtless as usual. Thither, Dundas, Pitt, and the " men " of the day, repaired—now for a day's rest—now for a night's fill of festivities and care-for-nought pastime—all dancing blindfolded on the precipice of destruction.

His parliamentary labours again over, he and Mr. Milner prepared (June, 1785) to rejoin the ladies they had left behind them in Italy. On the road thither, reading and examining the Greek Testament occupied the leisure of the two travellers; and the same employment we find them engaged in on the Rhine, in September of the same year—and, says our senator, " By degrees I imbibed Milner's sentiments, though I must confess with shame, that they long remained merely as opinions assented to by my understanding, but not influencing my heart. My interest in them certainly increased, and at length I began to be impressed with a sense of their importance. Milner, though full of levity on all other subjects, never spoke on this but with the utmost seriousness; and all he said tended to increase my attention to religion." " Often," he says, speaking of the free use he made of pleasure while at Spa, while in the full enjoyment of all that this world could bestow, " my conscience told me, that in the true sense of the word, I was not a Christian. I laughed, I sang, I was apparently gay and happy; but the thought would steal across me—' What madness is all this;' to continue easy in a state in which a sudden call out of the world would consign me to everlasting misery, and that when eternal happiness was within my reach! For I had received unto my understanding the great truths of the Gospel, and believed that its offers were free and universal, and that God had promised to give his Holy Spirit to them that asked for it. At length such thoughts as these completely occupied my mind, and I began to pray earnestly. As soon as I reflected sincerely on these subjects, the deep guilt and black ingratitude of my past life forced itself upon me in the strongest colours, and I condemned myself for having wasted my precious time, and opportunities, and talents. It was not so much the fear of punishment by which I was affected, as a sense of my great sinfulness in having so long neglected the unspeakable mercies of my God and Saviour; and such was the effect which this thought produced, that for months I was in a state of the deepest depression from strong conviction of my guilt. Indeed, nothing which I have ever read in the accounts of others exceeded what I then felt."

These extracts sufficiently show what the inward state of his mind was; but will he show his light? Will he conceal his new-born feelings and try to please God and mammon? Will the alarmed be still the gay young man, and mix in the frivolity of that company which to him was once so congenial? How will he treat, and be treated by, the fashionable world and those statesmen who had been his co-votaries in pleasure? Will he be "ashamed of Jesus"? Let him speak his own words and tell what his thoughts were at that time:—"Nothing so convinces me of the dreadful state of my own mind, as the possibility—which, if I did not know it from experience, I should believe impossible—of my being ashamed of Christ. Ashamed of the Creator of all things! One who has received infinite pardon and mercy, ashamed of the Dispenser of it, and that in a country where His name is professed!" The thin

line which was now the rubicon of the contending
combatants within him was to be passed—the struggle
was fierce, and well may we fancy we hear the
troubled senator crying

> "———Oh Thou my voice inspire
> Who touch'd Isaiah's hallowed lips with fire."

And in a few weeks he had grace given to him " to
make up his mind." He not only had felt the fullest
conviction that that happiness which he had been
enjoying was only like following a sound, and pur-
suing a dream; but he might have exclaimed in the
language of Cowper:—

> *   *   *   *   " Happiness,
>   I have sought thee in splendour and dress,
> In the regions of pleasure and taste :
>   I have sought thee, and seem'd to possess,
> But have prov'd thee a vision at last.
> " An humble ambition and hope,
>   The voice of true wisdom inspires ;
> ' Tis sufficient, if peace be the scope
>   And the summit of all our desires."

" Peace " was indeed his scope, and without more ado
he frankly and boldly made an avowal of the change
which God had wrought in his heart. To his friend
Pitt he considered it especially due that he should
open his mind. " I told him," says he, " that though
I should ever feel a strong affection for him, and had
every reason to believe that I should be in general
able to support him, yet that I could no more be so

much a party man as I had been before."—Some treated the announcement as the effect of a temporary depression, which social intercourse would soon relieve; one threw his letter angrily in the fire; others, knowing that his past life had not been vicious, imagined that he could but turn ascetic, and regretted the expected loss of his social accomplishments and political assistance. Another says, " Mr. Pitt, the great statesman, thought that his friend was out of spirits, and hastened to Wimbledon to cheer him, and to discuss him out of his fancies. He had looked up : and Divine strength and wisdom were not withheld from him. For two hours the friends discussed their differences. The man of the world tried to reason the young Christian out of his convictions, but soon found himself unable to combat their correctness, if Christianity were true." Mr. Wilberforce accounts for this in these words:— " The fact is, he (Mr. Pitt) was so absorbed in politics that he had never given himself time for reflection on religion."

But if his gay circle of friends were so much alarmed and astounded at the extraordinary change which they now saw had come over their once convivial companion, there was one who, more than any heard with astonishment and alarm the news of his reformation—that was that one who, when he was a child, hastened from Yorkshire to London to rescue him from what she deemed fanaticism: it was his mother. His letter to her announcing the great fact, breathes sentiments of pious affection, moderation, and resolution. "All," he says, "that I contend for is, that we should really make this book (the Bible) the criterion of our opinions and actions, and not read it and then think that we do so of course; but if we do this, we must reckon on not finding ourselves able to comply with all those customs of the world in which many who call themselves Christians are too apt to indulge without reflection." Neither in town nor country, nor in matters of business, did he intend to be a recluse. "No, my dear mother," he continues; "in my circumstances this would merit no better name than desertion; it is my constant prayer that God will enable me to serve him more steadily, and my fellow-creatures more assiduously; and I trust that my prayers will be granted, through the intercession of that Saviour 'by whom only we have access, with confidence, into this grace wherein we stand,' and who has promised that He will lead on His people from strength to strength, and gradually form them to a more complete resemblance of their Divine original." That mother was blest, doubly blest—blest in living to see her son a Christian, not in word only, but in deed—blest in having a son whose influence should be of so affectionate and valuable a nature as to be the instrument by which she herself was to become a Christian also—she happily lived to be of one mind with her son.

Mr. Wilberforce now turned Wimbledon Villa into what it was in his juvenile days—a Bethel. God's altar was again recognized where the knees of himself and aunt had often bent in humble supplication; and, where his youthful voice was heard in heavenly song, he and his friends Milner, Scott, Elliot, and Thornton, now bent before their Maker and lifted their voice of praise and thanksgiving to the God who had done such great things for him. London Clubs were given up, former friends who knew not God were treated with becoming respect, but their society avoided. Christian intercourse and friendship were now sought as eagerly as the pleasures of the world were before. While he did not "flee from man's pursuits and shun his ways," when business bade him draw near, he did not rush into the society of the worldling. He was now the man and the Christian, and

> " None acted both parts bolder—
> The man and Christian soldier."

The Christian Senator.

"Unrivall'd as thy merit be thy fame,
And thy own laurels shade thy envied name—
Thy name, the boast of all."

IN the Parliament of 1786, Mr. Wilberforce
stood in that august assembly as no longer the
gay and thoughtless M.P., but as a Christian
Senator. If his acts, as a member of the
House, were before characterized by honesty,
integrity, and independence, they are now to receive
an additional lustre, and proceed from motives
actuated by those higher principles which the spirit
of Christianity sets in motion in the bosom of her
disciples. The "love of Christ" was his talisman,
and that love continued to be the guide and rule by
which he henceforth discharged all his public and
private duties to the end of his days.

Christian love, like another well-known love, does
not always run smoothly. "While personally aim-
ing," writes one of his admirers, "at a higher

standard of character, his mind was deeply affected
by the corruptions of society around him. Their
depth and breadth, instead of overwhelming him
with despair, with which most men turn away from
contemplation of vast evil, aroused his whole renewed nature, and he conceived the bold idea of
becoming the reformer of his nation's morals." At
this period he was only twenty-eight, and yet we find
him writing at that time, " God has set before me,
as my object, the reformation of my country's manners." On one occasion, while travelling from
county to county, visiting the castles of the nobility
and the palaces of the bishops—arguing his project
of reformation with lords and prelates, in a spirit of
gentleness and unostentation, but with ardent zeal
and strong faith, devoid, however, of any enthusiastic
presumption—he was invited to stay on a visit to a
nobleman, who, in the course of conversation on the
subject of the corrupt state of the manners of the
masses, ridiculed the young Reformer's peculiar
notions. " So you," observed his host, " wish, young
man, to be a reformer of men's morals. Look then,
and see there what is the end of such reformers,"
pointing as he spoke, to a picture of the Crucifixion.
The nobleman could not have given a more effectual
illustration of the depravity to which *un*reformed
man had sunk, than by calling Wilberforce's attention
to the subject of that picture; if it was intended to

be a slur upon his Christian life, or to dampen his ardour, it had a contrary effect; it fanned the flame of zeal in the young man's breast—an appeal to the death of his Saviour, and the circumstances which brought about that death, effectually convinced Wilberforce that reformation was seriously needed, and that energies directed, and time devoted, in that channel, would not be misspent. Notwithstanding the many discouragements with which his new scheme was beset, and the opposition with which it met, it received the encouragement, approval, and co-operation of many, and ultimately performed much good service in its time and way; but his own personal example did more to impress men with the beauty and worth of a moral and Christian life, than all the good intentions of the society which he formed for that purpose. Hannah More bears testimony to this fact. "That young gentleman's character," she said, "is one of the most extraordinary I ever knew for talents, virtue, and piety; it is difficult not to grow wiser and better every time one converses with him." And we, of the present day, may re-echo these sentiments of that pious lady, and add of Wilberforce:—

> " The grave cannot thy virtuous deeds obscure,
> Thy life hath purchased to posterity
> An honest fame which ever shall endure."

But before we particularly notice that sublime

work,—to which he consecrated his political life—
the abolition of the slave trade, and to which we will
devote a special section,—let us take a brief review
of those events which were surrounding him, and a
short sketch of his political life in general.

While at home, Margaret Nicholson was attempting
the assassination of our sovereign, and both Houses
were engaged in the affairs of Warren Hastings, and
abroad, death was depriving Prussia of her Frederick,
and the smouldering spark was being fanned into
that flame which ultimately destroyed the Bastile
and brought Louis to the guillotine; while the report
was circulating that our own King was recovering
from madness, and throwing all shades of parties
into a kind of chaotic political confusion, and
Austria was declaring war against France; Gustavus
III., of Sweden, was falling by the hand of an
assassin, and Marat by the hand of Charlotte
Corday; while the blood of the gay and volatile
Marie Antoinette was mingling on the scaffold with
that of her soft and simple husband, and hostilities
were brewing, on the one side by England, Spain,
and Holland, and on the other by France, which
were to give victory to Lord Howe, and an opportunity for Jarvis, Duncan, Nelson, and Collingwood,
to carry our flag in triumph over every sea; while
Napoleon was signalizing his talents at Toulon, and
Wellesley was shattering the power of the formidable

Mahrattas in India; while Napoleon was being elected First Consul of France, and Ireland was being united to England; and, finally, while the latter part of the eighteenth century was being disgraced, and thousands ruined, by a land filled with speculators and loan contractors—till honesty nearly disappeared from the national character; and the effect of those momentous and disgraceful years was costing the country upwards of £500,000,000 of debt, and bringing us to the brink of bankruptcy and all the horrors which are the sure companions of debt, whether it fall on a nation or an individual: – during this notorious quarter of a century, the subject of our memoir stood in the British Senate-House an untainted member; and, with his judicious wisdom and cool discernment, aided, as a good and skilful mariner, to enable the captain of the bark of the British nation to weather the storms, and save her from a deplorable wreck.

The first important parliamentary matter in which we find him taking part in his new character, is in the case of Warren Hastings. On the motion for the impeachment of that gentleman in the above-named year, Mr. Wilberforce not only animadverted on the violence of zeal displayed by some members of the House of Commons on that occasion, but strongly recommended the Administration to exercise much circumspection and care before they allowed any papers to be produced, the publication of which might be prejudicial to the state.

Although, as I have remarked, a separate chapter will be devoted to the particulars relating to the abolition and emancipation of Slavery, some notice must be taken of it here, inasmuch as it forms the connecting link in his parliamentary career, and one by which he was distinguished as a member of the House of Commons.

It appears that Wilberforce was originally induced to move in the cause of humanity by the representations of Mr. Thomas Clarkson (the principal pioneer in the cause), whose views, at their first interview, he was disposed to question, and especially many of the allegations which that gentleman advanced in his *Essay on Slavery;* but after some investigation of the subject, he seems to have been satisfied of their truth, and at a dinner given by Mr. Bennet Langton, he formally agreed to become a member of a society which had been established with the view to put an end to the practice of making human beings articles of commerce. In consequence of the strong conviction he entertained on the matter, he in 1787 brought forward a motion relating to the abolition of the slave-trade, and which subsequently led to the presentation of petitions, in favour of that measure, from every part of the kingdom. Illness, however, prevented Mr. Wilberforce from proceeding in his good work, and therefore the next year Mr. Pitt, in the name of his absent friend, submitted some resolutions to the House. The business was, unfortunately, postponed to the following session, when the propositions were supported by the eloquence, not only of our philanthropist, but by that of Pitt, Fox, and Burke; and the question was carried without a division. But this was only like placing a straw across the Falls of Niagara, to stop the flow of its impetuous current. The object he had at heart had to contend with powerful and interested opposition; and in 1791, when he moved for leave to bring in a bill to prevent the further importation of African negroes into the British colonies, he was defeated, and the motion negatived by a majority of seventy-five. In 1792 he made another attempt, still supported by the (now rival) statesmen Pitt and Fox, and he so far succeeded as to induce the House to agree to a resolution for the gradual abolition of the abominable traffic in human flesh—a resolution which was carried with only eighty-five dissenting voices. The motto *Nil desperandum* still kept the hope of ultimate success alive; but it was not till 1807, during the short Administration that followed on the death of Mr. Fox, that Mr. Wilberforce had the gratification to see his labours effectual, to the extent of the abolition of the *trade* in slaves by subjects of Great

Britain. But let us retrace our steps to notice other matters relating to him in his duties as a member of the Legislature: and in scanning this part of his career, let us not forget how dangerous was the channel through which he and his fellow M.P.'s were sailing.

Mr. Wilberforce was usually to be found among the parliamentary supporters of Government, displaying, however, thorough consistency of conduct and firm adherence, both in the character of a Christian and legislator, to the principles he professed. In 1790, we find him declaring in favour of the conduct of Ministers, relative to the convention of Spain; and on the discussion of the war in India against Tippoo Saib, he asserted that that prince had been the original aggressor. He at first approved of the war with France, which followed the Revolution in that country; but he was likewise one of those who considered the continuance of the contest as impolitic after the establishment of a settled government there, and he consequently supported those who negotiated the treaty of Amiens. In 1804 he agreed to the propositions for inquiry relative to the defence of the country against foreign invasion; and in 1805 he displayed his independence in his conduct with regard to the accusation against Lord Melville, having, on June 11, made a motion for an impeachment of that nobleman, for high crimes and misdemeanours, which was lost, and an amendment by Mr. Bond was carried, directing the commencement of a criminal prosecution by the Attorney-General. It is said, that no less than forty members of the House were influenced by the speech of Wilberforce on the inquiry concerning the affairs of that statesman, and which Mr. Wilberforce considered as forming a proper subject of censure, while he could not but admit that his lordship had shown great ability while he headed the Board of Control over the government of India. In the course of his parliamentary career, he supported Catholic Emancipation and Parliamentary Reform; he reprobated lotteries as injurious to the morals of society, and asserted that the employment of boys of a tender age in the sweeping of chimneys was most intolerable cruelty. Shortly after the duel between Pitt and Tierney, he attempted, but in vain, to procure a legislative enactment against the practice of duelling; and in everything brought forward in the House tending to raise the moral and spiritual welfare of his nation, the voice and the energies of Mr. Wilberforce were sure to be found taking an independent and active part.

Wilberforce was the darling of his constituents. He was re-chosen, without opposition, for the county of York, at the elections in 1790, 1796, 1802, and 1806; but at that which took place in 1807 he had to encounter a powerful competition from the two great families of Fitzwilliam and Lascelles, each of whom are said to have expended the princely fortune of more than £100,000 in the contest. Possibly, some interested in electional matters may chance to read these remarks: it may interest them to know that purity of vote was an exception in 1800. They may tell to their elbow-neighbours, and to the utmost bounds of their electoral districts, that fifty years ago our countrymen in Yorkshire knew the rules of Cocker, as far as " Profit and Loss," when having reference to electional contests; that they, in that day, had some idea, as we have in ours, that money makes M.P.'s to go; that the worthy electors of Yorkshire knew quite as well the value of spade guineas, as many voters of the present day do the value of Victoria Sovereigns. The old member, however, was supported by a public subscription raised throughout the county, and he was again successful. The numbers of the voters, in this extraordinary contest, may be interesting to some. At the close of the poll, which lasted fifteen days, the numbers were as follows:—

William Wilberforce, Esq.	11,808
Lord Viscount Milton	10,990
Hon. Henry Lascelles	10,177

These formed the largest amount of voters which had ever been polled at a county election.

This contest did not pass without some severe comments from the enemies of the successful candidate, and consequently, Mr. Wilberforce deemed it requisite to vindicate his character by publishing a pamphlet, addressed to the freeholders of Yorkshire, wherein he confuted the insinuations, that he had, towards the termination of the combat, entered into a coalition with the party of the rival candidate, Mr. Lascelles. He also, at this time, addressed another pamphlet to the same persons, on the abolition of the slave trade. At the general election in 1812, Mr. Wilberforce—not being willing again to encounter the expense of another contest, the last, notwithstanding the subscription, having caused a very considerable reduction of his finances—retired from the representation, and was elected member for the borough of Bramber, in Sussex, for which he likewise had a seat in the two subsequent Parliaments, until, in 1825, he finally relinquished his senatorial honours, by accepting the stewardship of the Chiltern Hundreds. He had been then in Parliament forty-five years; and "during a part of that period," says one of his biographers, "his influence in the House was superior to that of any other individual not possessed of official power." Not only were his political opinions often the target for the arrow of sarcasms, but his Christian character was more than once made the object of attack by his pitiable antagonists. On one such occasion, when a popular member repeatedly, and contrary to that order which the discipline of the House enjoins, designated him as the "honourable and *religious* gentleman," Lord Brougham tells us that Mr. Wilberforce poured out such a strain of sarcasm which none who heard it can ever forget; "not because he was ashamed of the cross he gloried in, but," says his lordship, "because he felt indignant at any one in the British senate deeming piety a matter of imputation."—" A common friend of the parties having remarked to Sir Samuel Romilly, beside whom he sat, that this greatly out-matched Pitt himself, the great master of sarcasm, the reply of that intelligent and just observer was worthy to be remarked—' Yes,' said he, ' it is the most striking thing I almost ever heard; but I look on it as a more singular proof of Wilberforce's virtue than of his genius, for who but he ever was possessed of such a formidable weapon, and never used it.'" Reminding us of the well-known words:—

> " Thrice is he armed who has his quarrel just,
> And he but naked, though in triple steel,
> Whose conscience with injustice is corrupted."

Mr. Wilberforce is said to have possessed in perfection two of the most essential qualifications of a popular orator—the choice and most expressive purity of language, and the finest modulation of a sweet and powerful voice. The copiousness of diction which a classical education had conferred, and the ardent zeal arising from his religious sentiments and natural temper, contributed further to his excellence as a public speaker. One says, " The exclusive and limited system of opinions he had adopted, not merely with sincerity, but with passionate enthusiasm, rendered him earnest, vehement, and affecting, where a philosopher would be frigid and indifferent." And another observes (and these extracts are given in order that the reader may have *all* that is said of him by friends and foes : those living and who knew him personally will be able to judge to what extent credit may be awarded to these opinions), " Such is the extreme superiority of persuasive power which the partisan or the bigot will often manifest over the man of enlarged views and liberal opinions. That he was often *unconsciously* led into exaggeration, and indeed *unwillingly* to exceed the bounds of truth ; that he sometimes allowed his feelings to predominate over his reason, and hence led to ascribe unworthy motives [*i.e.*, in political matters] to those whose honour was as spotless as his own, cannot be denied ; but, on the other hand, he devoted all his energies to the cause of humanity, and to the advancement of those objects which, in his opinion, were likely to conduce to the moral improvement of mankind." But if we

"Nothing extenuate or set down aught in malice," we must sum up his parliamentary character in saying that he was an honest Christian man, and that, as such,

"Truth from his lips prevail'd with double sway."

Indeed, one, namely, Lord Brougham, who knew him personally both in his public and private capacity, and who is no mean judge of character, while in such matters his opinion carries the greatest weight, and is irrefutable wherever it is brought to bear, says of Wilberforce, that he was the "venerable patriarch in the cause of the slaves; whose days were to be numbered by acts of benevolence and piety; whose whole life had been devoted to the highest interests of religion and charity."

Let us again look outside:—from the year 1800, the period at which we closed our review of the scenes which were surrounding the outer life of Wilberforce,—let us here, before we revert to his private life, take up the subject and scan the events which had been passing during the quarter of a century which expired with his parliamentary career:—

"Jumping o'er time;
Turning the accomplishments of many years
Into an hourglass."

and it will shew that he lived in no ordinary times, but in times demanding hard parliamentary duties and profound forethought.

On the union of Ireland with England depended, in a great measure, the security of Great Britain, the circumstances attending which gave an opportunity for the secession of Mr. Pitt from the Ministry, and the appointment of Mr. Addington. While there was a union between the crown and its advisers, the war with France was continued to be prosecuted as before. While the defeat of the French at Alexandria, and the bombardment of Copenhagen by Nelson were lifting the spirits of the nation, the death of Sir Ralph Abercrombie cast a gloom over many at home, and the assassination of Paul I. of Russia no less astonished many in that empire, and rid the earth of a desperate despot; while the trident of Neptune remained in the hands of England, on the Continent Napoleon reigned supreme, and had crowded his armies towards the shore to invade our isle; while we stood in expectant attitude and prepared to give a warm reception to the enemy, should he escape the vigilance of our oaken bulwarks, both parties were made temporary friends by that treaty so unfavourable to Great Britain which was signed at Amiens on March 27, 1802—a treaty which at the end of thirteen months was cancelled by the acts of Napoleon. While the war was being renewed in 1803, Wellesley was fighting the battle of Assaye, and a republican government was being founded in Hayti. The next year 1804, Mr. Pitt returned to the Ministry, and on the Continent Bonaparte was made Emperor. While, in 1805, our immortal Nelson was gaining the crown of a victorious death at Trafalgar, and the French were capturing Vienna, and the battle of Austerlitz sending thousands to a premature grave, and the treaty of Presburg was being signed by France and Austria, at home the nation was busy with the impeachment of Lord Melville, and harassed by the news of the victories which Napoleon was daily gaining.

The death of William Pitt, 1806, was a great blow to the nation, and while Lord Granville, who succeeded him, was joined by Mr. Fox, and attempted to accommodate France, Napoleon was setting Louis Bonaparte on the throne of Holland, and Joseph on that of Naples, and receiving a check to his triumphs at the battle of Maida, under Sir John Stuart; while the kingdoms of Saxony, Bavaria, and Wurtemburg were being established, the nation was depositing the mortal remains of Charles James Fox by the side of his great rival in Westminster Abbey; while these two were being united by death and lamented by the living, the battle of Jena, and the capture of Berlin by Bonaparte, were calling our thoughts from the strife of death at home to the strife of nations on the Continent. In the next year, 1807, the Administration of " all the talents " signed its own death warrant with the same pen with which they had, a few hours before, that Act which gave to that Administration a glorious title of a martyr's crown, viz.: THE ABOLITION OF THE SLAVE TRADE.

While the Duke of Portland, with Mr. Percival, was at the head of the Ministry, the battle of Friedland was raging, Peace between France and Russia was signed, and the Danish fleet at Copenhagen seized by British tars. In 1808, while all the Northern Powers were intimidated by France, England stood alone — all Europe was banded against her, and led by Napoleon at the head of more than a million of men; Sir A. Wellesley was sent to aid Portugal, an expedition which gave the victories of Rolica and Vimiera to his laurels, and Sir John Moore received his death-blow at Corunna in the expedition intended to dethrone the usurper, Joseph Bonaparte, who had been transferred from Naples and made King of Spain by Napoleon on the abdication of Charles IV. In 1809, while a parliamentary investigation relative to the conduct of the Duke of York, as commander of the army, was going on, and Lord Castlereagh and Mr. Canning were settling their difference in a duel, Gustavus IV. was forced to resign the crown of Sweden, the Tyrolese were rising under Hofer, and the battle of Talavera was being won by our late " Iron Duke." The next year, 1810, saw Sir F. Burdett taken to the Tower; the divorce of Bonaparte from the Empress Josephine, and his marriage with Maria Louisa of Austria, and Holland annexed to the French empire. In 1811, the Prince of Wales became Regent, and the Spanish colonies in America independent. The next year, 1812, was an eventful one: while the indomitable spirit of the English—little helped by the cowardly allies—led by the immortal Wellington, rolled back the hosts of France from the Spanish territory, and sent them confused and broken across the Pyrenees, thereby adding to the roll of his victories the names of Badajoz and Ciudad Rodrigo; while Mr. Percival was falling by the bullet of Bellingham, and England was at war with the United States, Napoleon had set his foot on the neck of Europe, and was under the walls of Moscow — *in* Moscow, the city of the glorious Kremlin, with the tricolours of France waving triumphantly from its pinnacles, giving rule where an autocrat, not less tyrannical, had only a short time before been lord—*out* of Moscow, in flames, and making a disastrous retreat into interminable levels covered with snow—storms of snow and ice raging over the heads of the retreating and panic-stricken French, while a deadly enemy hovered over their flanks—till out of more than 500,000 men, only about 20,000 returned. That retreat was—

> " The carnival of Death;
> The vintage of the Grave."

The year 1813 gave to us the battle-crown of Vittoria, and saw a defeat of the Harasser of the European world at the battle of Leipsic. The means which tended to bring about this are graphically told—" This breathing time " (the armistice of Pleswitz, June 4, 1813), " was too good an opportunity to be lost by the British Cabinet. Sir Charles Stewart was sent over to the Continent with unlimited command of money. He bribed the German nations to be free; outbade Napoleon in Sweden; and paid the Czar of Russia for fighting in his own cause. Great Britain, like the benevolent uncle at the end of a comedy, distributed fortunes among all the personages of the drama. Sweden had two millions, and Prussia one, Russia one; and 80,000 Prussians, and 160,000 Russians were kept in British pay; and £5,000,000 of useless paper money was converted into solid gold by the credit of this country; and when Austria, awakened by the jingling of all this money, pretended to turn patriotic, in hopes of sharing the spoil, Napoleon was not blind to the motives of the coalition against him, and said to the Austrian Minister, ' Ah, Metternich! how much has England given you to make war upon me?' Satisfied with these benignant exertions in Germany, the Ministry neglected the army of Englishmen in Spain. While millions were flowing forth for the maintenance of half the faint-hearted kings in Europe, the forces in Portugal were in arrears of pay. The maritime support was weak and inadequate, and Wellington had to undertake the duties of commissary and financier as well as the commander in-chief. The fate, however, of Napoleon was now sealed. The same year saw the final crash of his empire at Leipsic and at Vittoria. In the first-named battle there were upwards of 400,000 combatants, with 2000 guns. Of these, 100,000 never left the field; and the French, who were outnumbered nearly two to one, were forced to a disastrous retreat, which exposed the territory of France itself to the invasion of the allies."

The year 1814 restored Ferdinand VII. to the throne of Spain; and while Paris surrendered, and Louis XVIII. was restored to his authority, the treaty of Paris was, on the 30th May, signed by the allied sovereigns and France. Bonaparte retired to Elba, and the treaty of Ghent, between Great Britain and the United States of America, gave a short respite to the war-trumpet of both the Old and New world. But this silence was not of long duration; in the next year, 1815 (the Glorious Year) the Holy Alliance was formed, Bonaparte escaped from Elba, landed in the south of France, marched to Paris, resumed the imperial power—the execution of Murat—and that which makes every Briton's heart jump with joy, was gained by the great Wellington — the Victory of Waterloo. Bonaparte abdicated, surrendered to the English, was deported to St. Helena, and the throne of France again restored to Louis. The events of this year form one of the most graceful feathers of pride in the cap of every British youth, and to old and young they are as familiar as " household words." While the year 1816 was ushered in by the death of the Queen of Portugal, and saw the Lord Exmouth's expedition start for Algiers, the marriage of the lamented Charlotte to Prince Leopold; that of the next year cast a deep veil of sorrow on the nation by the premature death of that amiable Princess; while this year, 1817, saw the completion of Waterloo Bridge, it is also noted for being the year in which Watson, Thistlewood, and others, were tried and acquitted for treason.

While abroad, in the beginning of the year 1818, death removed the King of Sweden from his throne; at home, the latter end of the same year is noted for the Congress of Aix-la-Chapelle, and saw the death of our own Queen, and those seditious movements which ended by a massacre of unarmed men and women at Peterloo, near Manchester. 1820 was ushered in by the decease of the father of our present beloved Sovereign, which event was shortly followed by the death of George III., and the accession of George IV., a Prince who, instead of devoting himself to the welfare of his people, sought his own personal convenience by enlarging his palaces and indulging in a loose and luxurious life. If his wife was ill educated and self-willed, she was treated with every indignity and insulted by every possible means that he and his servile courtiers could devise; but death in the following year released her from her troubles, and, if possible, withdrew the check which her life had upon his immorality. This year (1820) witnessed also the Cato-street conspiracy, and the execution of Thistlewood and his confederates; the treaty between Spain and the United States of America, and the cession of Florida: disturbances in Spain and Portugal, and the assassination of the Duke of Berri at Paris. 1821 may be called the " English black year," for it saw, in London, a riot around the funeral *cortège* of the Queen at the very time that her husband was exhibiting himself to his Irish subjects as a royal buffoon, feasting and making merry in the most thoughtless manner. If a bad man is a curse to his people, a King like George IV. is a thousand times more so to his subjects. In this year also died Napoleon Bonaparte at St. Helena. In 1822 the *Habeas Corpus* act was suspended; England and Ireland suffered great agricultural distress: famine and typhus broke out; and in Ireland the law was outraged in every province;

while O'Connell not only marshalled the excited millions, but deluded them with the most fallacious hopes.

Franklin returned from his expedition to North America; and the House of Lords was electrified by the news of the suicide of the Marquis of Londonderry. In 1823 the French invaded Spain, and the constitutional government of the country was subverted, while an attempt, in April of the next year, to depose the King of Portugal was defeated by the spirited conduct of the French and English Ambassadors. This year (1824) was also remarkable for the war between the British and Burmese in India; the death of Sir Charles Macarthy; and an insurrection among the negroes at Demerara, and in the West Indies. The year 1825, the year in which Wilberforce retired from parliamentary duties, was a remarkable year—there was the death of Ferdinand IV., King of the Two Sicilies, the accession of Francis I.; the death of Alexander, Emperor of Russia, renunciation of the Crown by the Grand Duke Constantine, and the accession of Nicholas I. of "sickman" notoriety and Crimean troubles. Great commercial panics in London; the recognition of the governments of Mexico, Columbia, and Buenos Ayres, by Great Britain, and a treaty of commerce by those States. Then, again, there was the convention between

England and Russia; the recognition of the independence of St. Domingo by France; the treaty between Great Britain and Brazil relative to the abolition of the slave-trade; and finally, by the wisdom of such men as had been at the head of affairs for the last few years, the nation prospered, notwithstanding the apathy of the crown.

Such is a brief outline of the events which surrounded the parliamentary career of Wilberforce from the year 1800 to the time he resigned his seat. I have been induced to give this short sketch for two purposes—to show, in connection with the life of Wilberforce, that a Christian life is not hindered by, or incompatible with, the duties which our country demands, though that person may be even a member of Parliament; and, secondly, to make this little book of some use (in addition to that which it furnishes as showing the life of Wilberforce to the rising generation), by supplying them with a summary of the events of the last twenty-five years, by which they may refresh their memory, or be guided in their reading for more extensive particulars. I will close these remarks by observing that, however varied and chequered the history of this said last quarter of a century may appear, it is quite true that, while we may find " sermons in stones and books in the running brooks," we may discover " Good in everything."

The Christian Gentleman.

"If meek humility e'er touched thy heart,
If deeds of charity thy soul revere,
If generous virtue can delight impart,
Reader, a monument of these is here!"

BEFORE taking special notice of the two important achievements to which Wilberforce more particularly devoted the best energies of his parliamentary and private life, let us briefly review his Christian career in private, previously to, and after he retired from, senatorial labours—and while quietly enjoying the peaceable life of a private gentleman, down to that day when a sorrowing Commons and a weeping public followed him, either in presence or thought, to the Abbey of Westminster —to that hour when, in ripe old age, he departed to cross that

"Bourn from whence no traveller returns."

In the year 1786, we saw our senator standing
in the House of Parliament as a Christian Legislator;
we have gone with him in that capacity through his
parliamentary career, and observed him surrounded
by, and taking part in, those events which fell to the
lot of his nation, unmoved in his Christian course
by the dangers and difficulties which were in-
superably connected with them; we have seen him
relinquishing his public duties with a character un-
spotted, and we have, moreover, heard what the
opinion of Hannah More—no mean judge of what
constituted the character of a Christian—was, in
reference to him shortly after he entered upon his
journey heavenward. It only remains, therefore, for
us, while striving to follow his good examples, to
take notice of those prominent traits which he
manifested in his subsequent days, for the benefit
of mankind, and which, at the same time, may serve
to illustrate the purity of his own life,—bearing in
mind that, as every Christian is, or should be, a light
to those among whom he lives, we may say of
Wilberforce that—

> His lamp was lighted
> To guide us on our way
> The heavenly pearls to find.

While Mr. Wilberforce's assiduity to his parliamentary duties, his conscientiousness, his talents,
and eloquence, were securing to him the respect and

confidence of both Houses of the Legislature, the purity of his life, the earnest with which he pleaded for a change in the morals of those around him, and his recognised disinterestedness of motives, prepared the public for those truths which flowed from his lips, and caused them to be admitted into many circles, from which either ignorance or hostility would otherwise have excluded them. The soundness of Mr. Wilberforce's moral and Christian life prepared men for the publication of that work, *A Practical View of the Prevailing Religious Systems of Professed Christians*, which was instrumental in awaking the lethargy of hundreds to a sense of their spiritual, or rather, non-spiritual condition, but particularly of being of signal use to that, then young, curate of Brading, in the Isle of Wight—who was afterwards known to the world as the author of the *Dairyman's Daughter*—namely, the Rev. Leigh Richmond; and also of engendering in Scotland's worthy Chalmers those spiritual sparks which to this day have made his name dear to the hearts of Scotia's pious sons. Of this work Mr. Wilberforce writes in his diary, 1793;—"Saturday, August 3, laid the first timbers of my tract."—When the house was subsequently completed, and ready for inspection by the public, many of his friends endeavoured to persuade him that it would never do to take such a course as making it public. The "timber" added to "timber," came out a book, the title of which we have already quoted. One of his friends wrote, "A person who stands so high for talent, must risk much in point of fame, at least, by publishing upon a subject on which there have been the greatest exertions of the greatest genius." Nothing daunted, to press the MS. must go, and the work stand or fall by its merits or demerits. He corrected the sheets during leisure intervals while attending committees of the House of Commons; and the index was the result of labour after midnight and wearying debates in the senate. Only five hundred copies were at first printed—such was the little demand for religious books at that time, that it was doubtful if half that number would find a sale. It was published April 12, 1797, and within a few days the book was not only out of print, but at the end of little more than half a year, it had seen five editions, or 7500 copies had been sold. How many copies have been disposed of since, it would be hazardous to guess. Bishop Porteus wrote of it:—"I am truly thankful to Providence that a work of this nature has made its appearance at this tremendous moment." His old friend Newton says:—"What a phenomenon has Mr. Wilberforce sent abroad! Such a book, by such a man, and at such a time! A book which must and will be read by persons in the higher circles, who are quite inaccessible to us little folks—who will neither hear what we can say, nor read what we can write. I am filled with wonder and with hope. I accept it as a token for good: yea, as the brightest token I can discern in this dark and perilous day. Yes, I trust that the Lord, by raising up such an incontestable witness to the truth and power of the Gospel, has a gracious purpose to honour him as an instrument of reviving and strengthening the sense of real religion where it already is, and of communicating it where it is not." It did all this, and even Burke with his dying breath, thanked the author through his physician. The work was "the produce of his (Wilberforce's) heart as well as of his understanding." This work solved the enigma which to many his altered life had propounded. " His condition as a layman saved him from the charge of professional bias; and a rich blessing from Heaven rested on his high endeavour to reach the heart in an ungodly age."

"Not a year passed throughout his after-life in which he did not receive (we are told) fresh testimonies to the blessed effects which it pleased God to produce by his publication. Men of the first rank and highest intellect, clergy and laity, traced to it their serious impressions of religion, and tendered their several acknowledgments in various ways—from the anonymous correspondent ' who had purchased a small freehold in Yorkshire, that by his vote he might offer him a slight tribute of respect,' down to the grateful message of the expiring Burke." To Mr. Pitt, Wilberforce sent a copy, directing his attention to the last section of the fourth chapter, and says, " You will see wherein the religion which I espouse differs practically from the common system." The portion of the section to which Wilberforce probably alluded was this:— " The grand radical defect in the practical system of these nominal Christians is their forgetfulness of all the peculiar doctrines of the religion which they profess: the corruption of human nature; atonement of the Saviour; and the sanctifying influences of the Holy Spirit!" It has been well observed, that if Yorkshire had no other monument of her honourable place in the rolls of her people, Wilberforce's *Practical View* would be of itself an ever-enduring memento of her existence.

It is only right to notice here, that the theological sentiments advocated in the *Practical View* are highly Calvinistic, and that occasionally it shows a slight tincturing of religious enthusiasm. Its merits, however, greatly preponderate, and its demerits vanish when they are judged by the test, that a truly Christian man wrote it, but not an infallible one. No truly Christian man will reject the *good* that one writes, merely because the writer differs with him on some peculiar point or other—

especially if the good (*i.e.*, taking a human view of
the matter) be not opposed to essentials in religious
doctrines ; that would be as praiseworthy as a
famishing traveller rejecting a draught of water
because it was not drawn from his own well. The
work provoked in its day the animadversions of the
Revds. Gilbert Wakefield and T. Belsham, of Dr.
T. Cogan, and some other opponents, whose whys
and wherefores we have not space for here. Shortly
after the publication of the *Practical View*,
Mr. Wilberforce, it appears, returned to Bath for a
while, and was there the observed and admired of
all observers and admirers ; but his reason and
modesty were not blighted by that which is pretty
frequently the misfortune to be the adhesive literary
plaister, namely,—vanity, and a love of being
deemed the *little Penates* of fashionable watering-
places and their hotels. While speaking of
Mr. Wilberforce's literary labours, we may take
notice here, that, besides the works already named,
he published *An Apology for the Christian Sabbath ;
An Appeal to the Religion, Justice, and Humanity of
the British Empire on Behalf of the Negro Slaves in
the West Indies ;* and was the author of *An Intro-
ductory Essay to Dr. Witherspoon's Treatises on
Justification*, &c., and contributed to the pages of
the *Christian Observer.*

For evidence of Wilberforce's inward feelings

about the time he published his *Practical View*, let us extract from his diary of Good Friday, April 4, 1779. "I thank God," he therein writes, "that I now do feel in some degree as I ought this day. I trust that I feel true humiliation of soul from a sense of my own unworthiness, a humble hope in the favour of God in Christ, some emotions from the contemplation of Him who at this very moment was hanging on the cross, some shame at the multiplied mercies I enjoy, some desire to devote myself to Him who has so dearly bought me, some degree of that universal love and goodwill which the sight of Christ crucified is calculated to inspire. Oh! if the contemplation here can produce these effects upon my heart, what will the vision of Christ in glory produce hereafter! I feel something of pity, too, for a thoughtless world! and oh! what gratitude is justly due from me (the vilest of sinners, when compared with the mercies I have received), who have been brought from darkness into light, and I trust, from the pursuit of earthly things to the prime love of things above. Oh! purify my heart still more by Thy grace. Quicken my dead soul, and purify me by Thy spirit, that I may be changed from glory to glory, and be made, even here, in some degree to resemble my heavenly Father." What inward peace do we see here enjoyed by one who, not many years before, turned not aside from sin's bedecked and flowery path. We may now say

" He was the freeman whom the truth made free."

On May 30, 1797, he married Barbara, the eldest
daughter of Isaac Spooner, Esq., a merchant of
Liverpool, and of Elmdon House, Warwickshire, by
whom he had four sons and two daughters. In
addition to his villa at Wimbledon he possessed an
estate at Markington, in Yorkshire, and was, for a
country gentleman, what is understood to be "well
to do"—not too rich nor too poor.

In 1808, Mr. Wilberforce took up his residence at
Gore House, Kensington. This mansion he made
his happy home. He found it, he says, more
salubrious than his house at Clapham; and writes
further, " We are just one mile from the turnpike at
Hyde Park Corner, having about three acres of
pleasure-ground around our house, or rather behind
it, and several old trees, walnut and mulberry, of
thick foliage. I can sit and read under their shade,
with as much admiration of the beauties of nature
as if I were two hundred miles from the great City."
Here he passed many years of his happy and useful
life; his house the resort of those men who awoke
our land from the deadly torpor into which years of
fearful warfare had plunged it. Here came Clarkson,
Zachary Macaulay, Romilly, and others, to commune
together on those measures which, to quote

Channing, brought about "the most signal expression afforded by our times of the progress of civilization and a purer Christianity." Wilberforce was exceedingly partial to Gore House, and his friends appear to have always found a ready home within it. Several of his friends died here. In 1814, Mr. Henry Thornton, for many years M.P. for Southwick, and one of his most earnest supporters, came hither for the benefit of the air and medical aid. He lingered a few weeks, and died here, January 17th, 1815, aged 53. Isaac Milner, too, an early friend, who came to London to attend the Board of Longitude, died here after five weeks' illness, on April 1st, 1820.

The following year Wilberforce quitted Gore House. He retired to Marden in Surrey, a lovely spot and an interesting locality; but he regretted leaving

"The still retreats that soothed his tranquil breast,"

and often in after years alludes to his old home, its associates, and his Kensington Gore breakfasts.

"Mild Wilberforce, by all beloved,
Once own'd this hallow'd spot,
Whose zealous eloquence improved
The fetter'd Negro's lot."

Often he had to exercise the difficult duty of self-restraint—sorely was that spirit tried which might have retaliated with the bitterest sarcasms; but he

had been under the tuition of a meek and gentle
Master—he could turn the shaft aside by his Master's
remedy—"bless and curse not"—"Turn to him the
other also." He was wont to meet his rampant
slanderers with—"Every animal employs the note,
or cry, or howl, which is peculiar to its species:
every man expresses himself in the dialect most
congenial to his temper and inclination, the most
familiar to the company in which he has lived, and
to the authors with whom he is conversant." His
more malignant and younger enemies he would
commiserate with :—"Poor fellow! I hope I can bear
him no ill will, but allow for, and pity him." Had
not Mr. Wilberforce been equally benevolent in his
private feelings, as in his public actions, he might
have become one of the bitterest satirists, and the
greatest wit of the century in which he lived.

Castlereagh's tragical death (August, 1822) peculiarly affected him. He says :—"Poor Castlereagh!
I never was so shocked by any accident. He really
was the last man in the world who appeared likely
to be carried away into the commission of such an
act, so cool, so self-possessed. It is very curious,"
he observes, "to hear the newspapers speaking of
the incessant application to business, forgetting that
by the weekly admission of a day of rest, which our
Maker has graciously enjoined, our faculties would
be preserved from the effects of this constant strain.

I am strongly impressed by the recollection of the endeavours to prevail on lawyers to give up Sunday consultations, in which poor Romilly (who destroyed himself in 1818) would not concur. If he had suffered his mind to enjoy such occasional remission, it is highly probable the strings would never have snapped as they did from over-tension."

About this period we have a beautiful illustration of the habits of two ages blending. Age and over-work were telling upon a naturally weak constitution, and now, in his later years, he often availed himself of the too frequent opportunities given by a heavy speaker, to indulge himself with an hour's sleep in the back seats in the gallery; and this indulgence was cheerfully and respectfully conceded by the House. To have disturbed the slumber of Mr. Wilberforce would have been with one consent scouted as "a breach of privilege," for which no ordinary apology would have atoned. Here is a beautiful little incident of old age and infancy :— Our beloved Queen does not of course, from her own knowledge, recollect who that playmate was, who, in 1820, was delighted with her innocent smiles and prattle. Wilberforce writes to Hannah More that in 1820 he was invited to visit the Duchess of Kent. "She received me," he says, "with her fine animated child on the floor by her, with its play-things, of which I soon became one." What a change since then! That "fine animated *child*" is now a *grand-mother* and our Queen, beloved by her people as never a sovereign was loved before! In reverence, reader, bow the head and pray God to bless and preserve her to us, and her husband and children to her, and bring her, them, and us, in His own good time, to those realms of bliss where we shall all be kings and princes in His Divine presence!

Mr. Wilberforce was, in his more domestic circle, also a man of prayer. Whoever surrounded his breakfast table—and persons of all ranks and the highest distinction were often there—was invited to join in family prayer. He was also a kind master, and when any of his servants were unwell, he would be found praying at their bedside. He likewise "Remembered the sabbath-day to keep it holy.' And we are told that, on one occasion, a Minister of State called on him on some public business on a Sunday; he at once excused himself, saying, he would wait upon his lordship at any hour he should fix the next day, but he was then going to church! And this was after he had already attended morning service. With Wilberforce let us joyfully say on each Sabbath :—

"Now let us repose from our labour and sorrow,
     Let all that is anxious and sad pass away :
The rough cares of life lay aside till to-morrow ;
     But let us be tranquil and happy to-day."

Not only was he the humble Christian and the ministering angel at the bedside of his own household in their sickness, but he extended his sympathies and the balm of consolation to the bedside of his friends and neighbours; wherever temporal and spiritual comfort were needed, there was to be seen the effects of the hand and heart of Mr. Wilberforce. Peaceable and gentle to all around him, in private life and in public, "fearful of giving," says Lord Brougham, "the least pain in any quarter, even while heated with the zeal of controversy on questions that roused all his passions; and more anxious, if it were possible, to gain over rather than to overpower an adversary; d sarming him by kindness, or the force of reason, or awakening appeals to his feelings, rather than defeating him by hostile attacks." His ethereal fire shone all the brighter when lighted to illuminate the erring steps of his private friends, and when Humanity breathed into his soul to invigorate his spirits on her behalf, "his eloquence," we are told on the same authority, "was of the highest order: it was persuasive and pathetic in an eminent degree" in general; "but it was occasionally bold and impassionate, animated with the inspiration which deep feeling alone can breathe into spoken thought, chastened by a pure taste, varied by extensive information, enriched by classical allusions, sometimes elevated by the more sublime topics of holy writ."

Dearly did he love and enjoy that retirement and that inward communion which is so beautifully described by Cowper. His soul imbibed the spirit, while his lips moved with the following words :—

> "The calm retreat, the silent shade,
> With prayer and praise agree,
> And seem by Thy sweet bounty made
> For those that follow Thee."

But we must now draw near to the time when the din and confusion of the battle of life were to be ended—when he should feel the blessed effect of having humbly leant upon his God. He had now for nearly fifty years been "posting" and "waiting", in the service of his Heavenly Master, stronger in spirit, though weaker in flesh, the eye of faith had been growing brighter and brighter as he drew nearer and nearer to that goal where the crown of glory and Christian victory were awaiting him as the reward of a long and persevering course in the paths of every Christian virtue. But, as if to give the strongest evidence that strength of spirit can strengthen the flesh, even though that flesh be on the eve of returning to "the dust from whence it was taken," we find Mr. Wilberforce only twelve weeks before his death, again appearing before the public. It was at Maidstone (near which he was residing at the time) on the occasion of a meeting to petition for the abolition of the West Indian slavery—the slave-trade, as we have already observed, having been abolished twenty years previously—there he appeared, his attenuated person buried almost beneath the cloak which protected him; his small frame had become smaller than ever, but his voice seemed to have been restored to that former clarion character with which he had aroused the slumbering energies of the senators—there he stood, supporting himself with his right hand on the table, and delivered his *last* public and dying words to the persons assembled in the Town Hall on that occasion. Venerable and pious,

> "His reverend lockes
> In comelye curles did wave;
> And on his aged temples grew
> The blossoms of the grave."

With a musical voice, and with the hand of death already upon his shoulder, he spoke:—" I had not thought to appear again in public; but it shall never be said that the tongue of William Wilberforce is silent, while the slave requires his help." Honoured indeed was the town of Maidstone by having had the presence of Wilberforce there on that occasion—doubly honoured was Maidstone in being the arena in which the last speech of the Slaves' Champion was delivered: and that speech, too, being on behalf

of the slave! Has Maidstone a monument of the
illustrious Wilberforce? No! The pedestrian, when
pacing that broad open street, cannot point to, and
ask of the inhabitants—Whose statue is that at the
top of your splendid street?—and receive the joyful
and welcome intelligence that, " it is the statue of
Wilberforce, the Christian, the Senator, and the
Slaves' Champion, which the inhabitants of our town
have raised to his honour and memory."

Those who saw him there must have recalled to
mind the words of the wise man—"The hoary head
is a crown of glory, if it be found in the way of
righteousness." He was most assuredly in that
" way," and that white hair was as a hallowed coronal
which graced his pure and Christian brow! From
the day he relinquished his seat in Parliament, he
could, in his retirement, enter fully into the spirit of
Milton's beautiful sonnet, and say:—

> " God doth not need
> Either man's work, or his own gifts. Who best
> Bear his mild yoke, they serve him best; his state
> Is kingly; thousands at his bidding speed,
> And post o'er land and ocean without rest;
> They also serve, who only stand and wait."

Towards the latter part of his days he removed
to Heighwood Hill, near Hendon, Middlesex;
and for a year or two before his death, his time was
principally passed at the house of one of his sons,
the Rev. Robert Wilberforce, of East Farleigh, near

Maidstone; or with another son (the present Bishop of Oxford), then Rector of Brixton, Isle of Wight. He was a good friend to the Institution known as the Lock Hospital, and frequently attended its chapel; in his "Diary" he often alludes to it, and Leigh Richmond mentions observing him at the Communion Table, on one occasion, with a negro at his side, a coincidence which, he afterwards found, was quite accidental. The incident was not without a lesson!

Two days before his death, the Bill for the Abolition of Slavery was read a second time in the House of Commons. He received intelligence of this—and it was the last public intelligence he was permitted to receive, before that most welcome of all—" Well done thou good and faithful servant. Enter thou into the joy of thy Lord!" On hearing the result of the Bill—"Thank God," he said, " that I should have lived to witness a day in which England is willing to give £20,000,000 sterling for the abolition of slavery." Often has he been heard to say, "After I have done all, I am still an unprofitable servant." What holy resignation did Mr. Gurney behold on that day, when he beheld him with uplifted hands declaring, "I have nothing whatever to urge, but the poor publican's plea, 'God be merciful to me a sinner!'" He was about to " enter into his rest."— The hour was approaching when he should calmly

say, " O death, where is thy sting ?   O grave, where
is thy victory ?" The friends around that death-bed,
looking, through flooded eyes, on that mortal frame
from which the vital spark was gliding unto Him
who gave it, must have recalled those beautiful
words of Blair :—

> " Sure the last end
> Of the good man is peace !   How calm his exit!
> Night-dews fall not more gentle to the ground,
> Nor weary worn-out winds expire so soft.
> Behold him in the evening-tide of life,
> A life well spent.   .   .   .   .   .
> By unperceived degrees he wears away ;
> Yet, like the sun, seems larger at his setting.
> High in his faith and hopes, look how he reaches
> After the prize in view !   .   .   .   .   .
>
> .   .   .   .
>
> Oh ! how he longs
> To have his passport sign'd, and be dismiss'd !
> 'Tis done ! and now he 's happy !   The glad soul
> Has not a wish uncrowned."

Yes, at Cadogan Place, Chelsea, on the morning
of Monday, July 29, 1833, then in the seventy-
fourth year of his age, he resigned his spirit into the
hands of his Saviour, in the sure and certain hope
of a resurrection to eternal life.   And Sir T. F.
Buxton says, " It is a singular fact, which marks the
hand of Providence, that on the very night on which
we were successfully engaged in the House of
Commons, in passing the Clause of the Act of
Emancipation—one of the most important clauses

ever passed, namely, ' Be it enacted,' &c., about the
time when these words were carried, the spirit of our
friend left the world! The day which saw the termination of his labours, also saw the termination of
his life." The announcement of his death was
received by the House of Commons with peculiar
feelings of sorrow. His friend and successor,
Mr. Buxton, was deeply moved; and while touch-
ingly expressing his love and admiration for the
character of Wilberforce, applied to him the
beautiful lines of Cowper:—

> "A veteran warrior in the Christian field,
> Who never saw the sword he could not wield;
> Who, when occasion justified its use,
> Had wit, as bright, as ready, to produce;
> Could draw from records of an earlier age,
> Or from philosophy's enlighten'd page
> His rich material—and regale the ear
> With strains it was a luxury to hear."

That hour which secured freedom for the slave
on earth, saw the immortal spirit of Wilberforce
soar to those realms of freedom where there is
" no more curse," where " the Lamb is the light
thereof," and where " His servants shall serve Him,"
" with Angels and Archangels," and where, " with all
the company of Heaven, he shall laud and magnify
His glorious name ; saying, Holy, holy, holy, Lord
God of hosts, heaven and earth are full of Thy
glory; Glory be to Thee, O Lord most High."

Let us, therefore, while we say, "Amen," and "Thy will be done," pray that " a double portion" of " the spirit" which Wilberforce possessed, may " fall on us" and on those who shall come after us!

Agreeably to his own direction, it was the intention of his family that he should be interred at Stoke Newington, in the vault belonging to the family of his brother-in-law, James Stephen, Esq.; but, in consequence of a public requisition from many noble and distinguished persons, his funeral took place at Westminster Abbey; his grave being near those of Pitt and Canning. And, reader, should you visit that sacred spot,

> Tread softly—bow the head—
> In reverend silence bow
> The head to God!
> Stranger! however great,
> With lowly reverence bow
> The head to God!
> For Wilberforce, the saint, lies buried there.

On August 22, 1833, a public meeting was held, at which the Lord Chancellor presided; when, among other resolutions, "it was determined that a subscription should be opened for the purpose of doing honour to the memory of Mr. Wilberforce, by the erection of a monument, and such other methods as may be calculated to promote, in connection with the name of Wilberforce, the glory of God and the good of mankind." Accordingly, a

beautiful statute of Wilberforce in his chair, on a
pedestal, was entrusted to the execution of
Mr. Joseph, and which was completed in 1840, and
now occupies a place in the north aisle of the
Abbey in which he lies buried. It is a beautiful
piece of workmanship: the very marble speaks the
benign and philanthropic spirit of the original.
The following inscription is on the pedestal:—

IN THE MEMORY OF
WILLIAM WILBERFORCE,
(BORN IN HULL, AUGUST 24TH, 1759.

DIED IN LONDON, JULY 29TH, 1833.)

FOR NEARLY HALF A CENTURY MEMBER OF THE HOUSE OF COMMONS,

AND, FOR SIX PARLIAMENTS DURING THAT PERIOD,

ONE OF THE TWO REPRESENTATIVES FOR YORKSHIRE.

IN AN AGE AND COUNTRY FERTILE IN GREAT AND GOOD MEN,

HE WAS AMONG THE FOREMOST OF THOSE WHO FIXED THE CHARACTER OF

THEIR TIMES,

BECAUSE TO HIGH AND VARIOUS TALENTS,

TO WARM BENEVOLENCE AND TO UNIVERSAL CANDOUR,

HE ADDED THE ABIDING ELOQUENCE OF A CHRISTIAN LIFE.

EMINENT AS HE WAS IN EVERY DEPARTMENT OF PUBLIC LABOUR,

AND A LEADER IN EVERY WORK OF CHARITY,

WHETHER TO RELIEVE THE TEMPORAL OR THE SPIRITUAL WANTS OF HIS

FELLOW MEN,

HIS NAME WILL EVER BE SPECIALLY IDENTIFIED

WITH THOSE EXERTIONS

WHICH, BY THE BLESSING OF GOD REMOVED FROM ENGLAND

THE GUILT OF THE AFRICAN SLAVE-TRADE,

AND PREPARED THE WAY FOR THE ABOLITION OF SLAVERY

IN EVERY COLONY OF THE EMPIRE :

IN THE PROSECUTION OF THESE OBJECTS

HE RELIED, NOT IN VAIN, ON GOD;

BUT IN THE PROGRESS, HE WAS CALLED TO ENDURE

GREAT OBLOQUY AND GREAT OPPOSITION,

HE OUTLIVED, HOWEVER, ALL ENMITY;

AND IN THE EVENING OF HIS DAYS,

WITHDREW FROM PUBLIC LIFE AND PUBLIC OBSERVATION,

TO THE BOSOM OF HIS FAMILY.

YET HE DIED NOT UNNOTICED, OR UNFORGOTTEN BY HIS COUNTRY;

THE PEERS AND COMMONS OF ENGLAND,

WITH THE LORD CHANCELLOR, AND THE SPEAKER, AT THEIR HEAD,

IN SOLEMN PROCESSION FROM THEIR RESPECTIVE HOUSES,

CARRIED HIM TO HIS FITTING PLACE,

AMONG THE MIGHTY DEAD AROUND,

HERE TO REPOSE,

TILL THROUGH THE MERITS OF JESUS CHRIST,

HIS ONLY REDEEMER AND SAVIOUR,

(WHOM IN HIS LIFE AND IN HIS WRITINGS HE HAD DESIRED TO GLORIFY,)

HE SHALL RISE IN THE RESURRECTION OF THE JUST.

The Abolition of the Slave Trade.

Slavery—Hell-born tyrant!
　　　　　Brave Albion
Hath snatch'd away thy key—
(To set thy pris'ners free)—
And made thee to stand,
　　　　Loath'd and condemn'd,
On her western strand,
　　　　A criminal—
Awaiting banishment!

ALTHOUGH the two great works of humanity and love—the abolition of the slave trade, and the subsequent emancipation of the slave—which occupied the best portion of the public and private life of Wilberforce, properly belong to the thread of the memoir, already given in the preceding sections, they could not conveniently or fully be noticed in those portions of his history, without some confusion to the seriatim incidents there recorded; consequently, the reader will have occasionally to allow his mind, while scanning the successive steps which he will observe were being made to bring about the accomplishment of these two glorious acts, to revert to the days to which they really belong, and over which they have shed a lasting lustre, while adding a glorious page in the history of Wilberforce, and an illustrated chapter in the annals of his nation.

Holy writ has proclaimed, through all times, from the days of Solomon, that "Righteousness exalteth a nation," and that "sin is the reproach of any people." If ever there was a crime, peculiarly a reproach to a people, it was that sin which man committed, and in which England acquiesced, of robbing his fellow-man of his freedom—of making him his beast of burden; lowering him below the cattle of the field; obliterating by tyranny and every species of cruelty which he could devise, that image which his Creator had declared was His "own likeness." For it is a fact that, to slave-owners, the less soul their *victim* possessed, the more their *animal* was worth to them; to them a praying negro was an idle negro!

> " The negro, spoil'd of all that Nature gave
> To freeborn man, thus shrunk into a slave ;
> His passive limbs, to measured tasks confined,
> Obeyed the impulse of another mind ;
> A silent, secret, terrible control,
> That ruled his sinews, and repressed his soul ;
> Where'er their grasping arms the spoilers spread,
> The negro's joys, the negro's virtues fled."

The horrors attached to slavery are too well known—would that an occasion had never been given to pen them!—to require any repetition of them here. Mrs. Stowe's work is familiar to tens of thousands; but the pictures she has drawn in her pages are only the shadows of the realities: no words, however artificially arranged, or facts of cruelty, however seemingly exaggerated, can at all convey the actual agonizing sufferings that the negro had in British West India, (and still has in other countries,) to endure. There is not a portion of scripture, referring to the sufferings of man, as mere man, that does at all depict negro sufferings. Why not? Because I imagine that the Divine Inspirator thought He had so positively commanded love, mercy, and justice, that the worst of men had sufficient to keep them (if they would) from acts of inhumanity. Slave owners would ignore Scripture if they could. But they cannot, though (and with shame I write it) backed by English journals and literary periodicals of the present day. Even that which is the nearest approximation to negro sufferings—" Men ride over our heads—we went through fire and water—hungry and thirsty our souls fainted within us"—and, Thou " broughtest us into the place of dragons—we were abhorred of men—no man cared for our souls," only touch the fringe of that suffering which was the cup of negro affliction; and, therefore, for us to attempt to paint that which, (however wanting in truth of delineation,) has been so often the endeavour of those who have been eye-witness of the subjects of their pictures, would be a task of fruitless supererogation; let us, rather, proceed to trace the steps by which, in the first place, ABOLITION was effected, and crowned subsequently by EMANCIPATION—subjects which must ever be living thoughts, in connection with the memory and times of Wilberforce, the Slaves' Champion, who was the instrument by which Great Britain was brought to let the negro

"Dwell a freeman in his fatherland."

Several years before Mr. Wilberforce took any part on the side of the slaves, there had been friends lifting their voice on behalf of their rights, endeavouring to obtain the ear of justice to execute true judgment between man and his oppressor. Among the first was Dr. Granville Sharpe, known as "the best and most eminent of mankind, and the first advocate of the negro." He quite accidentally became acquainted with the sufferings of a poor slave; after showing him all the humanity which his large soul so amply possessed, and devoting to his care the best attention which his medical skill so fully qualified him to give, the poor negro recovered; but was again claimed by his inhuman master; the right was disputed, the case brought before the judges, and decided in favour of the fiend in human shape. Granville Sharpe, feeling that the man had breathed English air, and that negro-slaves,

> " If their lungs
> Receive our air, that moment they are free ;"

published his case in 1769, and so influenced the hearts of his advocates, that when the case of another slave, George Somerset, was brought before Lord Mansfield, he, in 1772, reversed the decisions given in the former case, and gave judgment in these words :—"Immemorial usage preserves the memory of positive law, long after all traces of the occasion, reason, authority, and time of its introduction, are lost; and in a case so odious as the condition of slaves, must be taken strictly: tracing the subject to natural principles, the claim of slavery never can be supported. The power claimed by this return never was in use here. We cannot say the cause set forth by this return is allowed or approved of by the laws of this kingdom; and therefore the man must be discharged." This wise and righteous decision must have fallen on the ears of the blood-thirsty planters like a sudden and terrific thunder-clap: their blood, no doubt, boiled from its fountain to the extremest veins in their bodies, while their spirits sunk many degrees below zero in their inhuman barometer. It was the first blow struck at the whole system. It was not lost on the hearts of the friends of negro rights, and it served to open the eyes of the public to the cruelty and injustice of the planter. The "Society of Friends," who have been universally recognised for their commiseration in negro sufferings, as well as proving, more than once, friends indeed to friends in need, came forward as fellow-helpers. Dr. Peckard, in a sermon before the University, stigmatised the slave-trade as a "crime on a dreadful pre-eminence of wickedness—a crime which, being both of individuals and the nation, must some time draw down upon us the heaviest judgment of Almighty God, who made of one blood the sons of men, and who gave to all equal rights of liberty; and who, ruling all the kingdoms of earth with equal providential justice, cannot suffer such deliberate, such monstrous iniquity to pass long unpunished." The subsequent activity the doctor displayed in the same cause, fully proved that these words were not mere oratorical flourishes, but emanating from a heart that felt what his lips uttered. The germ was beginning to show its vitality, and the same doctor, when afterwards Vice-Chancellor of that University (Cambridge), gave the subject for a prize, " *An ne licet invitos in servitutem dare?*"—" Is it right to make slaves of others against their will?" This was, in every particular,

a new theme for the University-men of that day; it
needed little of classical lore, but a competent knowledge of all the bearings of the evils, the laws of
human usages, the origin of man's rights; it required that sympathy should not blind Justice,
while, on the other hand, Justice should not be
callous to the convictions of truth. "Is it right?"
implied an answer to the opposite, thus "Is it
wrong!" And so the challenge went forth. He
who won the prize tells the results of his labours,[1]
and has left a name as imperishable as that of
Wilberforce's. The winner was the young student
who is known to the friends of freedom as "the
venerable Mr. Clarkson, the pioneer of negro
freedom."

The subject of the slave trade was now more freely
discussed, and numerous friends warmly kept the
topic alive — pamphlets began to appear. "Six
'Friends' met in London as a kind of council, to
consider what step they should take for the relief
and liberation of the negro slaves in the West Indies,
and for the discouragement of the slave-trade on the
coast of Africa." They could do much in their own
quiet way; but they needed the strong hand of the
law to give *the* blow (neither of those six in council
was an M.P.), and that was not long wanting.

[1] See particulars in Mr. Thompson's speech in the *Birthday of Freedom*, at the end of this work.

Mr. Clarkson, who shortly joined them, interested our "Slaves' Champion," Mr. Wilberforce, as we have already seen in his memoir, in the good work —he whose character had already gained the highest respect of the House of Commons. He was their chosen mouth, and Mr. Clarkson, the agent and compeer by whom the weapons for the coming struggle were to be collected, set in order, and placed in the hands of the "Champion," to wield them to the death of the crying evil, and the dismay and terror of the grasping and inhuman planters. Mr. Clarkson went to work in right good earnest: his cause was just, and God opened up his path, and lighted him on his arduous and dangerous journey of love and humanity. He proceeded to Liverpool and Bristol, whence the traders sailed on their vile errand—he inquired into the character of the trade; he dived into the secrets of the traffic, and searched out besides the patent cruelties, those which only were known to the traders, the planter, and the poor negroes themselves. He did more: he sailed in a slave-ship with a cargo of the poor creatures, and there saw with his own eyes the facts which before he had only read of, or heard with his ears. He examined the interior of the ships, and the coffin-like space into which the poor victims were packed up for their voyage; and he handled, and examined for himself the barbarous shackles with which the limbs of the captives were loaded." So loathsome, that, to quote Shakespeare's words, " The very rats instinctively had quit it." And so he returned to his Champion, loaded with the materials, which, by self-denying and diligent labour, he had collected and provided for the onslaught.

While numerous good and true men outside were recruiting fresh soldiers for the ranks of S.F. [Slave-Freedom], and some publishing essays and other poems, which, like so many drums, should be the means of rallying many around the captains in the fight to give their "right hand to the hammer;" while from Land's-End to John-o'Groats, the land was ringing with anathemas against the horrid trade, and Mr. Roscoe was writing *A Scriptural Refutation of a Pamphlet lately published by the Rev. Raymond Harris* (a Spanish Jesuit, who had published a tract with the title of *Scriptural Researches into the Licitness of the Slave-Trade*), and *The Wrongs of Africa;* while he, by his energies, was laying (unlooked for) the planks which should lead him to honour at the general election of 1806— an honour which spoke the feelings of the men of Liverpool, while it conferred an honour on their new representative, who, because he was the friend of negro freedom, and had written against slavery, returned him at their sole expense *vice* General Tarleton, who had voted against the abolition of the slave-trade. I say, while Clarkson and his co-labourers were working

Like bees in sunny weather,

Mr. Wilberforce went to work in the hive, producing such a mass of undeniable facts and such voluminous testimony—clear as the mid-day sun in an unclouded sky, and with evidence stronger than the chains which bound the fettered slave, that the two great rivals, Pitt and Fox (as stated elsewhere) heartily and generously agreed to join him in the contest: they, as a matter of justice and policy; he, actuated by Christian principles, a brotherly love, and a firm conviction that while it benefited the negro, it would do honour to his nation. His feelings at that moment, when going to the House to fight for the slave, one would imagine Coleridge had made his theme, when he makes one to say:—

> "I therefore go, and join head, heart, and hand,
> Active and firm to fight the bloodless fight
> Of science, *freedom*, and the truth in Christ."

In the earliest years of his political life, the Champion was not without some high qualifications for conducting the cause of the oppressed; and it is even said that in boyhood he had *written*, for the daily journals, on the subject of the miseries endured by Afric's children. And now, among the great ones of Great Britain, there he stands *fighting* for the same children. He had already felt, in reply to "Who is my neighbour?" that it was said to him, though not exactly in the same words—"Thy neighbour is

> ————————yonder toiling slave,
> Fettered in thought and limb :
> Whose hopes are all beyond the grave ;—
> Go thou and ransom him."

Yes, in the words of one of his biographers— "His glowing and persuasive eloquence, his high political influence (rarely combined with independence), marked him out as fitted to achieve that deliverance for the oppressed, for which his generous mind would naturally long. Yet at this time he wanted that one requisite, without which all the rest would have proved insufficient. The statue, indeed, was framed with exquisite symmetry, but the ethereal fire was wanting. Personal ambition and generous impulses would have shrunk from the greatness of the undertaking, or grown wearied in the protracted struggle, and these hitherto had been the mainsprings of his conduct. 'The first year that I was in Parliament,' he said, 'I did nothing— nothing, I mean, to any good purpose; my own distinction was my darling object.' But now he acted upon a new set of principles: his powerful mind, his eloquence in speech, his influence with Mr. Pitt, his general popularity, were now all as talents lent to him by God; and for their due improvement he must render an account. Now, therefore, all his previous interest in the condition of the West Indian slaves led to practical exertion." In his memoir we have had the particulars of the several stages through which the object for which he was now struggling passed. The bill in 1791 was lost through the influence of West India interest. So bitter were his enemies against him, and so inimical were those whose illegal interests he was opposing, that planters, traders, and all who feared that the golden "goddess" being so spoken against, their "gain" would fall, maligned him to the fullest extent that tongues with such black hearts could unblushingly spread. Mr. Wilberforce himself says:—" So numerous were the slanderous insinuations which had been propagated by that tongue,

'Whose edge is sharper than the sword; whose tongue
Out-venoms all the worms of Nile,'

that—if they (the wrongs of the children of Africa) had not been true, nothing but a special Providence could have prevented my being hanged thirty years ago." Still nothing daunted, year after year the Champion renewed the contest, until the whole nation united, and made common cause with the Captain and the oft-defeated Champion, that the voice of the people for once echoed the voice of God,

and influenced the House, March 25, 1827, to
ABOLISH THE SLAVE TRADE FOR EVER. In other
words, (for let there be no mistake about the matter,)
England, as far as she was individually concerned,
washed *her* hands of the affair—no longer traded
herself in the abominable traffic, but left the sin to
be carried on by others. Still this was a step, and a
great one too, in the right direction:—

> " Quick at the call of virtue, freedom, truth,
> Weak withering age, and strong aspiring youth,
> Alike the expanding power of pity felt;
> The coldest, hardest hearts began to melt;
> From breast to breast the flame of justice glow'd;
> Wide o'er its banks the Nile of mercy flow'd;
> Through all the isle the gradual waters swell'd;
> Mammon in vain the encircling flood repell'd;
> O'erthrown at length, like Pharaoh and his host,
> His shipwreck'd hopes lay scatter'd round the coast."

I have above observed, that the sin is carried on
by others, and the following facts will bear me out
in this assertion, and show that a " Slaves'
Champion " is much needed in the circle in which
Brother Jonathan moves:—THE PRICE OF SLAVES :
—The *Richmond Dispatch* (United States) of July
[1859] includes, in its MARKET note, the traffic in
human beings in these words :—" In response to the
many inquiries made from persons at a distance as
to the prices slaves are commanding in the market,
we publish the annexed statement furnished by
reliable authority :—No. 1, men, 20 to 26 years old,

from 1450 dollars to 1500 dollars; best grown girls, 17 to 20 years old, from 1275 dollars to 1325 dollars; girls, from 12 to 15 years old, 1000 dollars to 1100 dollars; best ploughboys, 17 to 20 years old, 1350 dollars to 1425 dollars; boys from 12 to 15 years old, 1100 dollars to 1200 dollars. Likely families, and also boys and girls, command high prices, as there are several gentlemen" [*Gentlemen!* Jonathan look into an Englishman's dictionary for a definition of this word!] "in the market who are purchasing for their own plantations in the South."

The bounty Great Britain paid in the year 1858 on slaves and slave-vessels captured amounted to £15,000!!! According to intelligence brought by the mail steamer *Athenian*, news had reached Fernando Po that no less than 15,000 slaves have been shipped from the south coast of Africa during the months of April and May, 1860. The American steam-slaver which had been expected on the coast for a long time past, and for which the British cruisers had been on the look-out, had taken 1200 slaves on board, and got clear off, in spite of the "look-out" on the coast. The *New York Evening Post* says there are now eighty-five vessels known to be fitting out as slavers in that port alone. It declares that if the tolerance of the slave-trade is extended a little further, slaves will be landed in New York as freely as they are in Cuba.

The laws in Brazil in regard to slavery are benevolent, and aim at the emancipation of the slave. If a man have freedom, money, and merit, no matter how black may be his skin, no place in Brazilian society is refused him.

There is nothing so degrading to human nature or so characteristic of petty tyranny over, and cruelty to, each other as that shameful traffic, the Slave-Trade.

> " ——— Tyranny must be,
>   Though to the tyrant, thereby, no excuse."

Why, because a poor African has a colour different to an American, is he to be bought and sold at a public mart; brought with the scourge of tyranny and barbarous threats, to toil much harder than any Englishman's beast of burthen?—Is it because "Honest black disdains to change its colour?" If so, "Let the white man blush."

If the American will not even eat or drink with a free negro—scarcely sail in the same ship with him—can we suppose that he will treat the negro slave tenderly! The Americans, with some few exceptions, say—" Were you to live among them (the slaves), you would hardly look upon them as better than beasts of burthen; their brutish appearance, their sordid and slavish dispositions, would make you imagine them scarce to be a link of the great chain." Oh! free-born Americans, had Heaven pleased to have given you Afric's sooty hue, and fixed your lot there, your sentiments would have been widely different. You would curse the "Institution" that reduced you to such a degradation, and legalized the right of another to your body and soul.

There are some humane masters of slaves who are more like fathers and mothers to their slaves, and who by their kindness have attached their slaves to them, so that, if offered freedom, they would not have it; but the majority are such as to cause the poor negroes to deplore their slavish condition, complain bitterly of cruel lashes for trivial offences, and almost to prefer death to toil and servitude under them. If an American can't get a honest penny without the slave-trade and its "Institution," let the avaricious owners at least treat their slaves with tenderness and compassion; let them reflect, that every blow they give them they must answer for at the great and awful bar of that high tribunal, where every one will be rewarded according to his doings; and where the poor and oppressed hireling and slave will perhaps enjoy a state of ease and bliss far above the proudest tyrant:—

> "Where no Fiends torment, nor Christians
> Thirst for Gold."

When a man boasts of the dignity of his nature, and the advantages of his station, and then and from thence infers his right to oppress his inferiors in natural advantages—whether blessed with a white or "cursed" (so say the pro-slavery party) with a black skin—he exhibits his folly as well as his malice. And when one sees *Literary Journals* disgrace their pages with critiques advocating Slavery, or "lashing" those who advocate Freedom, all that can be said for the writers, in extenuation, is, that they *abuse* the freedom with which God has blessed them. This brings to my mind the saying of one, who, while expressing his anxieties for the welfare of his fellow-men, said, "I observe with pain that there is an unwholesome tendency visible in the composition of some *Literary* Journals of the present day, and especially an attempt to spread pro-slavery principles, and to 'cut up' the advocates of Freedom in language most ungentlemanly, coarse, and vulgar —an attempt, under the garb of a *Review*, to (would-if-they-could) say something witty, which, when analyzed, is the poorest of poor adulteration."—"I tell you," he continued, "that if I wished (as I most certainly do) to bring up my son as a *Christian gentleman*, I would not allow him to read *Tom Paine* nor the *Literary Gazette*; but I would put the *Bible* and the *Athenæum* into his hands." How far the character of these two *Literary Journals* correspond with the foregoing remarks, the reader must judge for himself. In the *Athenæum* one never reads— however severe the critiques may be—anything but the most gentlemanly language. In the *Literary Gazette*————but " Comparisons are odious "— besides, " a boomerang is a dangerous weapon in unskilful hands."

Every person untainted with pride, and unbiassed by prejudice, sees and acknowledges this incontestable truth, that the Supreme Being is wise, and just, and good, and merciful; and every sensible Christian must acknowledge that it is his duty to be, in his acts to his fellow-man, as much like his Creator as possible. There is no man of feeling, that has any idea of *justice*, but would confess, upon principles of reason and *common sense*, that if he were to be put to *unmerited pain* by another man, his tormentor would do him an act of *injustice*. Now, a man of feeling and justice will not do so; because he will not do that to another which he is unwilling should be done to himself. Nor will he take any advantage of the accidents of fortune to abuse them to the oppression of his inferiors— blacks or whites—he knows that in the article of *feeling* all men are equal. Superiority of intellect, locality, rank, or station, is intended to communicate happiness to all our race : it can give no right to tyrannize over, nor to inflict unmerited pain. Unless God has given the strong man a right to knock down the weak man, the tall man to trample the dwarf under foot, the *white man* has no right to enslave and tyrannize over the black man. It has pleased God the Father of all men to cover some men with white skins, and others with black skins; God has made both, given both immortal souls—and there is neither merit nor demerit in the colour of skin : both are men, both are accountable beings, and both are bound to love one another; to act by each other as each would were the circumstances and colour of the skin of each reversed. Whether a man be white or black, fair or brown, tall or short, rich or poor, such he is by God's appointment. I am not ashamed, as a Christian, to be on the side of those who advocate the bettering the negro's con-dition; neither am I ashamed to testify that, in every shape and form, I utterly abhor slavery. The Benevolent Creator, the Merciful Jesus, the Benign Comforter,—the Bible of the Great God,—commands, both by example and precept, to *show mercy, to love justice, and to love thy neighbour as thyself.* The Wise Man says:—" There are many devices in a man's heart, nevertheless the counsel of the LORD that shall stand." Prov. xix 21. Let every Christian remember the negro and the slave when in that beautiful Litany he prays:—" From envy, hatred, and malice, and *all* uncharitableness; from hardness of heart, contempt of God's word and command-ment, Good Lord deliver us."

I will conclude this chapter with the following

pathetic poem by *Cowper*, as applicable to the Slave-Trade carried on by America and Spain at the present day:—

The Negro's Complaint.

Forc'd from home and all its pleasures,
    Afric's coast I left forlorn,
To increase a stranger's treasures,
    O'er the raging billows borne.
Men from England[1] bought and sold me,
    Paid my price in paltry gold;
But though their's they have enrolled me,
    Minds are never to be sold.

Still in thought as free as ever,—
    What are England's[1] rights, I ask;
Me from my delights to sever,
    Me to torture, me to task?
Fleecy locks, and black complexions,
    Cannot forfeit Nature's claims;
Skins may differ, but affections
    Dwell in black and white the same.

Why did all-creating Nature
    Make the plant for which we toil?
Sighs must fan it, tears must water,
    Sweat of our's must dress the soil.

[1] The subject of this poem does not *now* apply to England.

Think, ye masters, iron-hearted!
   Lolling at your jovial boards,—
Think how many backs have smarted
   For the sweets your cane affords.

Is there, as ye sometimes tell us,
   Is there One who reigns on high?
Has He bid you buy and sell us,
   Speaking from His throne, the sky?
Ask Him, if your knotted scourges,
   Fetters, blood-extorting screws,
Are the means which duty urges
   Agents of His will to use?

Hark! He answers:—wild tornadoes,
   Strewing yonder sea with wrecks,
Wasting towns, plantations, meadows,
   Are the voice with which he speaks:
He, foreseeing what vexations
   Afric's sons do undergo,
Fix'd their tyrants' habitations
   Where His whirlwinds answer—No.

By our blood in Afric wasted,
   Ere our necks receive the chain,
By the mis'ries which we tasted,
   Crossing, in your barks, the main;

By our suff'rings since you brought us
    To the man-degrading mart,
All sustain'd with patience, taught us
    Only by a broken heart;

Deem our nation brutes no longer,
    Till some reason ye shall find
Worthier of regard, and stronger
    Than the colour of our kind.
Slaves of gold! whose sordid dealings
    Tarnish all your boasted powers,
Prove that you have human feelings
    Ere you proudly question our's.

Emancipation and Freedom.

The Creator on High, marked that boon as 'twas given,
And smiled on its donors approval from Heaven.

PROPHETICAL were the words of the pious Clarkson, when, on the acquirement of Abolition, he said:—"There are yet blessings which we have reason to consider as likely to flow from it. Amongst these, we cannot overlook the great probability that Africa, now free from the vicious and barbarous effects of this traffic, may be in a better state to comprehend and receive the sublime truths of the Christian religion. Nor can we overlook the probability that a new system of treatment necessarily springing up in our islands, the same bright sun of consolation may visit her children there."

He continues: "But here a new hope rises to our view. Who knows but that emancipation, like a beautiful plant, may, in its due season, rise out of

the ashes of the Abolition of the Slave-trade; and
that, when its own intrinsic value shall be known,
the seed of it may be planted in other lands? And,
looking at the subject in this point of view, we
cannot but be struck with the wonderful concurrence
of events, as previously necessary for this purpose,
namely, that two nations, England and America,
should in the same month, in the same year, have
abolished the impious traffic: nations which, at this
moment, have more than a million of subjects
within their jurisdiction to partake of the blessing."
And yet, most extraordinary, that at *this moment*
(1861) America has millions of her subjects groaning
under the chain of slavery. When viewing the
present state of affairs in America (in the [dis]
United States), one cannot but be struck with the
almost prophetic sentiments uttered by Mr. Jefferson,
the President. Jefferson was himself a slave-owner,
and full of the prejudices of slave-owners, yet he left
this memorable testimony: " I do, indeed, tremble
for my country, when I remember that God is just,
and that His justice may not sleep for ever. A
revolution is among possible events." This needs
no comment. Had Jefferson lived till now, he
would behold his fellow-countrymen plunged in all
the horrors of internal revolution. Yes, Jefferson
would now see that " God is just." When shall
America exclaim—Justice *before* Interest?

Repentance, feigned there can be no doubt, had nearly put a veto on any further progress on the road to freedom. A better treatment of the slave was put forth as a barrier which was to stop the necessity for any more interposition of the negro's friends in England; and, indeed, those friends " had early agreed to limit their political action on this subject, to the abolition of the trade."

Probably the slave-owners in some instances saw the imperious necessity of a new and better system, that matters might not be carried further; and it is right to state that the masters (with some exception) did treat their slaves better than before the Abolition Act passed; but the real owners did not always live on their estates, and the poor negro was too often left to the tender mercy of the overseer, of whose brief authority it is said:—" Not only did the task-master torture the bodies of the vassals by the whip, but he also corrupted their morals by his licentious-ness. There was no law either to guard the chastity of a female slave, or to avenge any insult that might be offered to her violated honour. Nay, more—an attempt on the part of a slave to protect his wife, his mother, or his daughter, from such insult, might be punishable with death. Thus, as they had no protection in their domestic intercourse, so neither had they any security in their sympathies and sorrows."

" While their oppressors, as caprice or passion

dictated, could inflict upon their wretched victims
sufferings almost beyond endurance, a slave who
raised his hand by nature's instinct for his own
protection, or struck, or threatened to strike, or used
any violence towards, or compassed or imagined the
death of a master or mistress, was doomed to suffer
death, without benefit of clergy. On the other hand,
the murder of a slave by a white man was a venial
offence, and, from the inadmissibility of slave
evidence, often escaped punishment altogether. The
slave was, therefore, entirely unprotected from the
tyranny of his master, nor could he be a party
in any civil action, either as plaintiff, defendant,
informant, or prosecutor, against any person of free
condition. Thus he was protected only as an
inferior animal. Should he be maimed by a free
person, the damage would not be awarded to him,
but to his master."

So long as this treatment was liable to be adopted,
abolition was of little intrinsic value, and consequently, although missionary labour had done and
continued to exercise its beneficial effects on the
condition of the slaves, still there was that something wanted which should make a good and
satisfactory completion to the work begun, and it
was " Black man, be Free ! " Is the convicted thief
allowed to retain the property he has stolen ? And
can it be righteous, if the trade in slaves be unjust,

to permit the holders of human property, to retain that property which by unjust means they have acquired? Certainly not! And so said the negroes' friends; but, as in the former case, when abolition was first mooted, the case wanted a parliamentary champion. Wilberforce was not dead, but he was going, by the weight of years and infirmity, gradually to God who is our Home. The chariot and horses were almost in sight, and the spirit had been already caught by Sir Thomas F. Buxton.

The following letter was the first that Wilberforce wrote to Buxton, his future ally and successor. It may be deemed almost prophetic :—

"KENSINGTON GORE, *November* 28, 1816.

"My dear Sir,—I must in three words express the real pleasure with which I have both read and heard of your successful effort on Tuesday last, in behalf of the hungry and the naked. . . . But I cannot claim the merit of being influenced only by regard for the Spitalfields' sufferers in the pleasure I have received from your performances at the meeting. It is partly a selfish feeling, for I anticipate the success of the efforts which *I trust you will one day make in other instances*, in an assembly in which I trust we shall be fellow-labourers, both in the motives by which we are actuated and in the objects to which our exertions will be directed.—I am, my dear sir, yours sincerely,   W. WILBERFORCE."

Again Wilberforce wrote to his successor:—

"LONDON, *May* 24, 1821.

"My dear Buxton,—It is now more than thirty-three years since, after having given notice in the House of Commons that I should bring forward, for the first time, the question concerning the Slave Trade, it pleased God to visit me with a severe indisposition, by which, indeed, I was so exhausted, that the ablest physician in London of that day declared that I had not stamina to last above a very few weeks. On this I went to Mr. Pitt, and begged of him a promise, which he kindly and readily gave me, to take upon himself the conduct of that great cause.

"I thank God I am now free from any indisposition; but from my time of life, and much more from the state of my constitution, and my inability to bear inclemencies of weather, and irregularities, which close attendance on the House of Commons often requires, I am reminded, but too intelligibly, of my being in such a state that I ought not to look confidently to my being able to carry through any business of importance in the House of Commons.

"Now for many, many years I have been longing to bring forward that great subject, the condition of the negro slaves in our Transatlantic colonies, and the best means of providing for their moral and social improvement, and ultimately for their advancement to the rank of a free peasantry—a cause this, recommended to me, or rather enforced on me, by every consideration of religion, justice, and humanity.

"Under this impression, I have been waiting, with no little solicitude, for a proper time and suitable circumstances of the country, for introducing this great business; and, latterly, for some member of Parliament, who, if I were to retire, or to be laid by, would be an eligible leader in this holy enterprise.

"I have for some time been viewing you in this connection; and after what passed last night, I can no longer forbear resorting to you, as I formerly did to Pitt, and earnestly conjuring you to take most seriously into consideration the expediency of your devoting yourself to this *blessed service*, so far as will be consistent with the due discharge of the obligations you have already contracted, and in part so admirably fulfilled, to war against the abuses of our criminal law, both in its structure and its administration. Let me, then, entreat you to form an alliance with me, that may truly be termed holy, and if I should be unable to commence the war (certainly not to be declared this session); and still more, if, when commenced, I should (as certainly would, I fear, be the case) be unable to finish it, do I entreat that you would continue to prosecute it. Your assurance to this effect would give me the greatest pleasure—pleasure is a bad term—let me rather say, peace and consolation; for alas, my friend, I feel but too deeply, how little I have been duly assiduous and faithful in employing the talents committed to my stewardship; and in forming a *partnership* of this sort with you, I cannot doubt that I should be doing an act highly pleasing to God, and beneficial to my fellow-creatures. Both my head and heart are quite full to overflowing, but I must conclude. My dear friend, may it please God to bless you, both in your public and private course. If it be His will, may He render you an instrument of extensive usefulness; but, above all, may He give you the disposition to say at all times, 'Lord, what wouldest thou have me to do, or to suffer?' looking to Him, through Christ, for wisdom and strength. And while active in business and fervent in spirit upon earth, may you have your conversation in heaven, and your affections set on things above. There may we at last meet, together with all we most love, and spend an eternity of holiness and happiness complete and unassailable. Ever affectionately yours,

W. WILBERFORCE."

Many causes had been concurring to prepare Mr. Buxton for entering upon this holy enterprise, and in March, 1823, he brought forward a resolution in the House of Commons, "declaring that slavery was repugnant to the principles of the

British constitution and the Christian religion, and that it ought to be gradually abolished throughout the British dominions." But interests here, like Plutoan guards, stood in the way. Mr. Canning's sketch—one of the simplest as well as one which it was thought the planters would have at once been glad to have adopted—was rejected with disdain (not, of course, without the sanction of parties at home behind the scenes), and when his bills were suggested, insinuations were thrown out that probably, if attempted to be enforced, the Islands, and especially Jamaica, might be put under the protection of the American flag. Mr. Canning's bills were intended to carry out an extensive line of amelioration, as will be seen from the sketch :—"To establish an officer to be called the Protector and Guardian of Slaves—To admit and regulate the evidence of slaves in civil and criminal cases—To regulate proceedings for obtaining the manumission of slaves—and to enable them, under certain restrictions, to purchase their freedom —To regulate the celebration of marriages among slaves, to declare such marriages valid and effectual in law—To suppress public markets on Sundays, and to prevent slaves being compelled to labour on that day—To enable slaves to acquire property, and to make provision for the safe keeping of such property, by the establishment of savings' banks—

To prevent the separation of slaves, being members
of the same family, by virtue of any legal process—
To give additional regulations for the punishment
of slaves, whether such punishment was inflicted
in due course of law, or by the authority of the
owners."

The slaves, notwithstanding the excuses, could
not be kept in utter ignorance of the influence
which their friends in England were endeavouring
to bring to bear on their behalf. The slaves were
anxious, and the masters held angry discussions,
which ultimately led to the rising of the slaves in
1831, and in a very short time property to a very
large amount was destroyed on nearly two hundred
estates; the canes at this season being so much
advanced, and surrounded with dry leaves, were
easily set on fire, and burned so rapidly as, in the
darkness of night, to illuminate the neighbouring
mountains. But, though scarcely any blood appears
to have been shed by the slaves, it is computed that
about two thousand of them lost their lives.

The missionaries were blamed as having been
instrumental in these revolts; but, without entering
into all the particulars of the accusations, &c., let
us hear what the Earl of Ripon (then Viscount
Goderich) says on the subject, when writing to the
Earl of Belmore:—"The documents which your
lordship has transmitted, ascribe the recent commo-

tions, not merely to the erroneous belief among the slaves that some new law had set them free, but to the influence of religious instruction, communicated by ignorant teachers, and received by a population unprepared by previous education to apprehend the real spirit of Christianity—assuming that Mr. Annand" (the person whose evidence as overseer had been laid before the writer) " correctly understood, and that he has correctly quoted, the language of the insurgent slaves, and that they spoke the common sentiments of the whole religious society of which they were members, this part of the general subject becomes of the highest importance.

" Among those who acknowledge the Divine authority of our national faith, there is no room for controversy respecting the duty of imparting the knowledge of Christianity to all mankind, and especially to our own more immediate dependants. However the modes or seasons of instruction may be regulated, according to the various circumstances of different classes of society, nothing can justify the systematically withholding from any men, or class of men, a revelation given for the common benefit of all. I could not, therefore, acknowledge that the slaves of Jamaica could be permitted to live and die amidst the darkness of heathen idolatry, whatever effect the advancing light of Christianity might ultimately have on the relation of master and slave;

nor am I anxious to conceal my opinion, that a change in this relation is the natural result of the diffusion of religious knowledge among them. For, although the great moral virtue of contentment and universal benevolence may be expected to appear among a Christian slave population, as the legitimate fruit of Christian principles, yet all probability justifies the belief, and all experience attests the fact, that the increased range of thought, the new habits of reflection, and the more lively perception of the duties owing by their fellow-Christians to themselves, to which the converted slaves will attain, will gradually produce in their minds new feelings respecting their servile condition.

"It is also well worth while to reflect on the inevitable tendency of the laws for the abolition of the slave-trade. So long as the islands were peopled by importations of native Africans, who lived and died in heathenism, the relation of master and slave might be expected to be permanent; but, now that an indigenous race of men has grown up, speaking our own language, and instructed in our religion, all the more harsh rights of the owner, and the blind submission of the slave, will inevitably, at some period more or less remote, come to an end.

"Deeply impressed with this conviction, his Majesty's Government have endeavoured to make timely preparation for a change, which they believed could not be made abruptly, without desolation and general ruin; and the calamity which we have at present to deplore is but an additional proof of the necessity of acting on so delicate a subject with this provident foresight; and of repressing those unhappy heats and prejudices, which have so long obstructed the advance of this indispensable improvement, both of the law and the state of slavery.

"I am not disposed to deny that the work of religious instruction may, in some instances, have been undertaken by men ill qualified for so arduous a task; and I am even ready, for the sake of argument, to adopt the improbable supposition, that the pure truths of Christianity may occasionally have been adulterated by instructions of a seditious nature; assume this to be the case, and what is the proper inference? Not, assuredly, that the slaves should be left to their native superstitions and idolatry, but that renewed exertions should be unremittingly made to diffuse among them more just apprehensions on religion, and clearer views of those moral obligations to the enforcement of which all Christian instruction should be subservient.

"It is not, however, merely to a misconception of religious truth, but to direct instigation of some of the missionaries, that the recent insurrection is ascribed, in some of the documents which your lordship has transmitted. I must distinctly avow my conviction, that the improbability of the charge is so extreme, that nothing short of the most irresistible evidence could induce a belief of it. The missionaries who engage in the office of converting the slaves in our colonies, cannot, with charity or justice, be supposed to be actuated by any views of secular ambition, or personal advantage. They devote themselves to an obscure and arduous and ill-requited service; they are well apprised that distrust and jealousy will attend them; and that the path which they have chosen leads neither to wealth nor reputation. If in their case, as in that of other men, motives less exclusively sacred than those which are avowed may exercise some influence on their minds, it were irrational either to feel surprised, or to cherish suspicion on that account. The great ruling motive must be that which is professed: since, in general, there is no other advantage to be obtained than the conscientiousness of having contributed to the diffusion of Christianity throughout the world."

The base attempts by which the slave-owners sought "to secure the perpetuity of their system proved the cause of its destruction;" and now was the pivot receiving the last revolution of the difficulty on that smallest of all pivot-points,—"We shall see,"—which, as one voice, arose to determine

which should prevail. " Christians of every denomi-
nation, patriots, and philanthropists of every rank
and name, simultaneously arose, and determined
not to be resisted or delayed; that liberty
immediately and unconditional, the birthright of
every man, should at once be enjoyed by Africans and
their descendants, throughout the British dominions,
equally with other subjects of the realm."

At a public meeting convened to petition, in
1830, for the *gradual* abolition of slavery, Dr.
Andrew Thompson moved as an amendment, that
Emancipation should be *immediate;* his amendment,
was triumphantly carried, and his speech on that
occasion is worthy of being handed down from
father to son.   He spoke:—

" Taking into account the circumstances of the
free blacks—their number, their wealth, their loyalty,
their general character—every one must see that
we may safely look to that portion of the West
Indian community as standing between the colonists
and all danger that may be apprehended from the
emancipation of the slaves; and, coupling this
with other considerations, it does appear to me that
we have the amplest security for that measure—
how soon soever it may be carried—being as
bloodless and peaceable as our hearts could desire.
I have no fear—no, not the shadow of it—that any
of the dreaded mischiefs will ensue from the course

of proceeding that we are pressing on the Legislature. In my conscience, I deem them all chimerical, and got up chiefly for the purpose of deterring us from insisting on that act of simple but imperative justice, which we call upon the British Parliament to perform.

"But if you push me, and still urge the argument of insurrection and bloodshed—for which you are far more indebted to fancy than to fact—thus I say, be it so. I repeat that maxim, taken from a heathen book, but pervading the whole Book of God, *Fiat justitia — ruat cœlum.* Righteousness, sir, is the pillar of the universe. Break down that pillar, and the universe falls into ruin and desolation. But preserve it, and though the fair fabric may sustain partial dilapidation, it may be rebuilt and repaired —it *will* be rebuilt and repaired, and restored to all its pristine strength, and magnificence, and beauty. If there must be violence, let it even come; for it will soon pass away;—let it come and rage its little hour; since it is to be succeeded by lasting freedom, and prosperity, and happiness. Give me the hurricane rather than the pestilence. Give me the hurricane, with its thunder, and its lightning, and its tempest;—give me the hurricane, with its partial and temporary devastations, awful though they be; —give me the hurricane, with its purifying, healthful, salutary effects;—give me that hurricane, infinitely rather than the noisome pestilence, whose path is never crossed, whose silence is never disturbed, whose progress is never arrested, by one sweeping blast from the heavens; but which walks peacefully and sullenly through the length and breadth of the land, breathing poison into every heart, and carrying havoc into every home, enervating all that is strong, defacing all that is beautiful, and casting its blight over the fairest and happiest scenes of human life—which, from day to day, and from year to year, with intolerant and interminable malignity, sends its thousands and its tens of thousands of hapless victims into the ever-yawning and never-satisfied grave!"

Again, in 1831—O'Connell, at a public meeting, spoke as follows on colonial slavery; and he, as well as the former speaker, declare the minds of the middle and lower classes, and are given in connection with the names of the great ones of the day, to show the universal feeling which inspired the heart. O'Connell said :—

"No man can more sincerely abhor, detest, and abjure slavery than I do. I hold it in utter detestation, however men may attempt to palliate or excuse it by differences of colour, creed, or clime. In all its gradations, and in every form, I am its mortal foe. The speech of an opponent on this question has filled me with indignation. 'What,' said this party, '*would you come in between a man and his freehold!*' I started, as if something unholy had trampled on my father's grave, and I exclaimed with horror, 'A freehold in a human being!' I know nothing of this individual; I give him credit for being a gentleman of humanity; but if he be so, it only makes the case the stronger; for the circumstance of such a man upholding such a system, showed the horrors of that system in itself, and its effects in deceiving the minds of those who are connected with it, wherever it exists. We are told that the slave is *not fit* to receive his freedom—that he could not endure freedom without revolting. Why, does he not endure slavery without revolting? With all that he has to bear, he does not revolt now; and will he be more ready to revolt when you take away the lash? Foolish argument!

"But I will take them up on their own grounds— the ground of *gradual* amelioration and preparation. Well; are not eight years of education sufficient to prepare a man for anything? Seven years are accounted quite sufficient for an apprenticeship to any profession, or for any art or science; and are not eight years enough for the negro? If eight years have passed away without preparation, so would eighty if we were to allow them so many. There is a time for everything—but it would seem there is no time for the emancipation of the slave.

Mr. Buxton most ably and unanswerably stated to the House of Commons the awful decrease in population; that in fourteen colonies, in the course of ten years, there had been a decrease in the population of 45,801—that is, in other words, 45,801 human beings had, in that period, been murdered by this system—their bodies gone to the grave—their spirits before their God. In the eight years that they have had to educate their slaves for liberty, but which have been useless to them—in those eight years, one-twelfth have gone into the grave murdered! Every day, ten victims are thus despatched! While we are speaking, they are sinking—while we are debating, they are dying! As human, as accountable beings, why should we suffer this any longer? Let every man take his own share in this business. I am resolved, if sent back to Parliament, that I will bear my part. I purpose fully to divide the House on the motion, *that every negro child born after January* 1, 1832, *shall be free.* They say, O do not emancipate the slaves suddenly; they are not prepared, they will revolt! Are they afraid of the insurrection of the infants? Or, do they think that the mother will rise up in rebellion as she hugs her little freeman to her breast, and thinks that he will one day become her protector? Or, will she teach him to be her avenger? O no! there can be no such pretence.

"I will carry with me to my country the recollection of this splendid scene. Where is the man that can resist the argument of this day? I go to my native land under its influence; and, let me remind you, that land has this glory, that no slave-ship was ever launched from any of its numerous ports. I will gladly join any party to do good to the poor negro slaves. Let each extend to them the arm of his compassion; let each aim to deliver his fellow-man from distress. I shall go and tell my countrymen that they must be first in this race of humanity."

Consequently, on the 14th of May, 1833, a motion was made in the House of Commons, to bring slavery to an end. The Act—that "*first-class*" Act, passed the British Parliament; an Act which sheds immortal honour on all connected with its successful achievement; an Act which stands among other bright acts on the statute-book of British Liberty, and as one of the most glorious to be found among the statutes of England's law and England's Freedom. A great day was that 14th of May, 1833, and a greater still was that 1st of August, 1834, when the negro of our British possessions called himself "*his own in Christ:*" when he should be a free man—free as God made Adam free—free, only that now he had gained freedom of body and mind, he was to be in bonds of love which should bind him

more closely to his brother on earth, and his
"Brother," Creator and Redeemer, in heaven.

The Friends of Freedom in that day might
have said:—

Slavery!

The decree, Median-like, is sealed;

The edict is gone forth,

Thy power from Ind to blot.

Pleadings fail now to allot

E'en a day's respite.

Yon setting sun shall not see

The execution of that decree:

At midnight it shall be done—

Slav'ry banish'd ! Victory won!

It's done;

Allelujah ! Praises to the Lord

Are sung,

And welcome the Orient Orb

Rising on

FREEDOM.

Glorious, indeed, must have been that day! It
was the removing of that last stone on which the
West Indian Bastile had so long stood to the
disgrace of this country. It placed on the heads of
Clarkson, our Champion, and their compeers a crown
of victory more valuable than that which Victory
placed on the brow of the "Hero of a hundred
fights." Long, long will that day's deeds be among
the "Living Thoughts" of the West Indian negroes,
and be cemented to the honour of Wilberforce and
all the friends of freedom who took part in bringing
it about.

My MS. originally contained a much larger account of the deeds with which the recollection of that day is associated; but since the revision of my notes and the MS. was ready for the press, the Birthday of Freedom has been celebrated; I have therefore struck out much which I found agreed with the speeches delivered on that occasion, preferring to append an account of that day's proceedings, and an outline of what was said (by many from experience), to anything I had written.

It has been beautifully observed that, " On the page of history, one deed shall stand out in whole relief—one consenting voice pronounce—that the greatest honour England ever attained was when, with her Sovereign at her head, she proclaimed,— THE SLAVE IS FREE; and established in practice, what even America recognizes in theory, that all men are created equal—that they are endowed by their Creator with certain unalienable rights—that amongst these are life, liberty, and the pursuit of happiness."

Who, even at this day, has a soul capable of being touched with that feeling which excessive joy gives, does not feel that the bare repetition of the joyous acclamations which rang among the thousands, and were echoed from earth to the heavens, and from the skies back to the caverns in that now free soil—who, I say, does not feel the

emotions arise at the sound of "Freedom":
"Freedom is come," "We be free, we be free; our
wives and children—we all be free"? Yes, thousands
do; and now truly may we say:—

> "Great was the boon, my country, when you gave
>   To man his birthright, freedom to the slave;
>   Rights to the wrong'd, and to the glorious rolls
>   Of British citizens a thousand souls;
>   Their glowing minds from slavery's slough to lift,
>   And make them worthy of the God-like gift!"

While Bishops and Missionaries tell of the blessed
effects freedom has had in promoting the spiritual
and moral welfare of the freed negroes, Mr. Gurney
gives an illustration of what it has done in a social
point; it needs no comment—those who run may
read. He says:—"As I was riding down the
Mandeville Hills, enjoying the grandeur of nature,
and the beauties of cultivation, I overtook a good-
looking young negro, handsomely attired, and
mounted on a pony of his own. He was a labourer
on Richmond Park coffee estate, in the parish of
Charendon; paid half a dollar per week for his rent;
was able to earn four dollars per week, by piecework;
had paid £10 sterling for his pony; kept wine, at
times, in his cottage; had gone to Mandeville to
obtain his marriage certificate from the rector; and,
with his young bride, seemed to be in the way of as
comfortable a measure of moderate prosperity as

could easily fall to the lot of man. This is one specimen among thousands of the good-working of freedom." Why, there is many a white lady in England who would jump at such a prospect as this free negro offered to his bride, and say nothing about his colour; for depend upon it where love is, it looks below the skin—to the heart; and who shall be so bold as to say the black man has not so good and noble a heart as his white brother? The fair reader will, I trust, pardon this little concluding remark, and join the poet in singing:—

"Friends of the outcast! view the accomplish'd plan,
The negro towering to the height of man.
Now justice leagued with mercy from above,
Shall reign in all the liberty of love;
And the sweet shores beneath the balmy west,
Again shall be 'the island of the blest!'"

The Birthday of Freedom.

That ENGLAND—the FREE—broke the chain of the slave,
(Thus set an example to all who'd be brave,)
Shall waft over seas, and re-echo on shore—
Our sons shall repeat it till time be no more.

* * * * * * * * * * *

We'll praise Thee—great Author of *freedom* for all—
The deeds of our WORTHIES, with love we'll recall—
Like silver bells ringing—sweet musical sound,
We'll tell of the Blessings the Negro has found.

THE following interesting evidence of that spirit of gratitude—due to God and man —which is still living in the hearts and memories of many of the present generation for the bringing about of that glorious work of Slave Emancipation a quarter of a century ago; and of those undying energies which are still being exerted on behalf of universal negro freedom, have been extracted from the public journals, and the crude notes of the author of the foregoing pages— who, rejoices to be able to add, was one of the audience on the day in question—a day on which the hearts of the hundreds present, (in the Music Hall,

Store Street, London,) to celebrate the Twenty-fifth
Anniversary of the Birthday of the Freedom of
Slaves, must have overflown with rapturous delight
at seeing the chair, on that occasion, filled by one
who is known to the world as the most erudite man
of our age, and the illustrious and worthy successor
in that cause which the lamented, but ever-to-be-
remembered, Wilberforce, long, patiently, and
successfully espoused. The particulars of that
day's meeting abound with encouragements ; and
the speeches delivered are so interesting, that the
author of this work, (which was in MS. on that day,
and nearly ready for the press,) feels that he needs
only name the source from which the extracts are
taken (viz., the *Times*, the *Star*, and some two or
three other papers) to command respect for the
veracity of the report. The subjects which engaged
the attention of the ears and hearts of the audience
on that afternoon, are worthy of being recorded in a
form which, it is hoped, will be of a more lasting
character than that which the pages of our numerous
journals afford. Newspaper reports are, to a certain
extent, ephemeral—so far as the eye is affected ; but,
on the other hand, subjects recorded in books have
a better chance of coming more frequently under the
notice, and, consequently, of making a more lasting
impression on the memory of a reading community.
Let me trust, therefore, that these reasons will

be deemed a sufficient apology for appending to this work the extracts, &c., of the speeches delivered on that Twenty-fifth Birthday of Freedom ; and, further, venture to hope, that while my readers are engaged in perusing the following pages, their hearts will be moved to aid in the good work, and their own examples spread around, to all mankind, the sweet perfume of a useful and consistent Christian life, coupled with feelings of humanity and brotherly love, so that their acts may be like

> Roses and Lilies—
> Emblems of the Beautiful—the Pure, and
> The Free.

Notice of the Meeting.

"BIRTHDAY of FREEDOM to EIGHT HUNDRED THOUSAND BRITISH SUBJECTS.

"THIS DAY (Monday), August 1, 1859, a PUBLIC MEETING to celebrate the Twenty-fifth Anniversary of the Abolition of Slavery in the British Colonies, will be held in the MUSIC HALL, Store Street, Bedford Square. The Right Hon. Lord BROUGHAM will preside. *   *   *

An Anticipatory Leader of the " Star," August 1st.

"Twenty-five years ago this day, there took place one of the greatest events in the history of England —an event which exalted this nation high above the other civilized nations of the earth, while it gave birth to numerous communities of free men. We refer to the Act of Emancipation, which exactly a quarter of a century ago took effect in the West India Islands, amid universal shouts of rejoicing on the part of the eight hundred thousand human beings upon whom it conferred the blessing of personal freedom. We are not yet able to realize the grandeur of this great act of national justice, nor can we yet foresee the influence which it will exercise upon our own destiny, and upon that of the hundreds of millions of the African race. It is enough for us to know that by the abolition of Negro Slavery in our own colonies, we wiped away the foulest stain upon our national escutcheon, elevated to the dignity of free men every human being within the wide limits of the British empire who had previously been held in a state of bondage, and prepared the way for those anti-slavery movements in France, Holland, Portugal, Brazil, and the United States, which, although they have as yet been only partially successful, will assuredly one day result in a triumph as signal as that which we have achieved.

"And is it not right and fitting that if there are saints' days and holy days, which are devoutly remembered and kept throughout this great England of ours—the 1st of August, the anniversary of the emancipation of the West India slave, should also be set apart as a day on which Englishmen should rejoice in the recollection of the most glorious event in our modern history, and nerve their arm for the struggle in which they have yet to engage on behalf of the holy cause of freedom? There is not an Englishman—probably not even a West Indian planter—who will not emphatically declare that so great an event should receive a noble commemoration.

"We are happy, then, to announce that, at one o'clock this day, 'the birthday of freedom to eight hundred thousand British subjects' will be celebrated by a public meeting, to be held in the Music Hall, Store Street, Bedford Square. Lord Brougham, the most illustrious of living Abolitionists, will appropriately preside; and when we remember that during his public life, of between fifty and sixty years, he has waged unceasing war against 'the wild and guilty phantasy that man can hold property in man,' and that during that lengthened period he has taken a leading part in all the movements for the abolition of slavery and the slave-trade, we can well conceive what the noble orator to-day will find it in his heart to utter. Lord Brougham, will, doubtless, be surrounded by many who took part with him in those great conflicts, and the world will see that their ardour in this cause has not abated, while they will know that there are some upon whom their mantles will descend when they have departed.

The speeches of the day will be delivered by the Hon. Francis Hincks, the Governor of Barbadoes, and Mr. George Thompson. Mr. Hincks, one of the most enlightened of our colonial governors, can testify to the glorious results which have flowed from emancipation in that portion of the West India islands with which he is best acquainted. Nor has any man a better right to review the results of West India emancipation, or to explain the nature of the work which has yet to be done, than Mr. George Thompson, who has been, for nearly thirty years, the eloquent advocate of the slave, and has confronted more mobs, and incurred more personal peril on behalf of the cause of emancipation and of free speech, than perhaps any other living man. To the testimony of these men will probably be added that of the Hon. Amasa Walker, of Massachusetts, who is well qualified to represent the anti-slavery sentiment of the United States, not only as a member of the Republican party, but as a man who has always expressed his earnest sympathy with the ultra-Abolitionists of the country from which he comes.

"We hope that the meeting to-day will inaugurate a revival of the anti-slavery cause in this country. There are signs and tokens of danger in this country which render such a revival necessary. There is a traffic in which Englishmen are engaged—a traffic which receives the sanction of law, and is justified in high places, that presents many points of resemblance to the slave-trade. And, further, there are not wanting indications of a desire, not indeed to re-enslave the negro, but to surround him by such a mass of heathenism, and by such a modified system of slavery, as cannot fail to stand in the way of his improvement, and to prevent the great moral results which emancipation was calculated to effect, and which, to some extent, it has already produced. The time has, therefore, come when the friends of freedom must combine to jealously guard the rights of the enfranchised negro, and to prevent the British flag from being polluted by the slave-trade in any form whatever. It is not free labour or free immigration which we are called upon to oppose, but a traffic in men, which is not less the slave-trade because its advocates have not the honesty to designate it by its right name.

"We hope that to-day the names of those great champions of the slave who have disappeared from the scene of their labours will not be forgotten. The names of Clarkson and Wilberforce, Buxton and Sturge, should especially be remembered. Fitting homage should be paid to their memories, because history demands this tribute of respect, and because their names are a talisman still powerful enough to rekindle the enthusiasm with which they lighted up all England."

THE MEETING OF AUGUST I, 1859.

(Extracted from the " Star," " Times," &c.)

BIRTHDAY OF FREEDOM IN THE WEST INDIES.

A PUBLIC meeting was convened yesterday at one
o'clock, at the Music Hall, Store Street, Bedford
Square, to celebrate the Twenty-fifth Anniversary
of the Abolition of Slavery in the West Indies—
The Right Hon. Lord Brougham in the chair.

Lord BROUGHAM in opening the proceedings,
after briefly acknowledging the enthusiastic reception which greeted him upon taking the chair, said,
—It naturally gives us all great satisfaction that we
have lived to see accomplished this great measure
of slavery abolition, than which there was none in
the whole history of our career at all superior in
importance or in virtue, or in what may be expected
to be its beneficial consequences, and that we have
now, by the goodness of Providence, been spared
to witness the twenty-fifth anniversary of that great
event, a quarter of a century to-day having elapsed
since the shackles of the slave were finally struck
off. I ought not perhaps to say " finally struck
off," for there was substituted for slavery an
indentured apprenticeship of seven years, which in
many respects, was only a mitigated form of the
evil which we had crushed, and which our utmost
efforts were forthwith applied also to terminate. I

derive unspeakable satisfaction in looking back to the year 1838, when I led in the contest for diminishing the period of apprenticeship by two years. It had then existed five years, but instead of continuing till 1840, it ceased in 1838; and I will do the Colonial Legislatures the justice to say—having oftentimes been in opposition to them, and, from various misapprehensions which are incidental to all controversies, having been greatly misunderstood by them—that they themselves by their own acts, under the suggestion of us from the Imperial Parliament, operating upon the Imperial Government, reduced the period of apprenticeship by two years. They therefore, I rejoice to say, are fellow-labourers with us in that great good whereby the 1st of August, 1838, finally witnessed the complete and absolute emancipation of our slaves. If there is any thing that gives me pain on the present occasion, it is, in the first place, that our example has not been followed by other countries ; that Spain particularly, which is the worst of all in many respects, notwithstanding the influence which we ought to possess—not by reminding her of benefits conferred, but by simply noting to her that we were fellow-labourers in her independence of France,—that Spain, I say notwithstanding our natural and just influence, has not followed that example—nay, has not completely abandoned the slave traffic, carried on in spite of treaties as well as of all honesty and honour. But, by degrees, truth will prevail over even Spanish counsels, and they will find that their own best interest—indeed, I would add, their safety in the West Indies—consists in extending to Cuba the measure of emancipation. I grieve to say that our brethren, our kinsfolk in America, furnish another exception to our example; but of that I would speak tenderly, from recollecting that America has acted admirably in many respects, and even abolished the slave-trade a year before we ourselves did it. Even in Georgia, which is as devoted to the "institution," as they are pleased to call it, as any of the Southern States, it was our fault, and not theirs, that they ever had slavery, for we pressed it upon them, and they refused it. They protested against it, but we defeated them; and it is our fault that that "institution" prevails in those States. But it is pleasing to reflect that our reasoning, and the reasoning of our public men, as well as of our diplomatic agents, may probably succeed there and in Spain also, so that we shall see the end of that abuse, and slavery will be no more:—

> "O spread thy reign, fair peace,
>   From shore to shore,
>   Till conquest cease,
>   And slavery be no more."

I need not remind you that friends of liberty are also friends of peace, and that they who have the greatest abhorrence of slavery are they who most justly and most earnestly detest war. But I have said that the feeling of satisfaction with which one meets upon the present occasion is dimmed by more than one recollection, and I chiefly mention the melancholy consideration that we here meet so few of the old patriarchs of the cause. They have gone long since, many of them very long since, and some more recently, to their account—an account certainly rendered more safe for them, and more edifying to us, by the purity of their lives, and by the great value of their public works, and of no one part of their lives, and no one portion of their works, more than by their having done their endeavour, and with success, to abolish the African slave-trade, and to free the African slave. I remember the absence here of such men as Wilberforce, as Clarkson, as Stephen, as Macaulay, and last but not least, of Joseph Sturge, whom we lately lost, and an irreparable loss it was. Of Wilberforce, the great champion of our cause, in Parliament and out of Parliament, I will only say, in the words which I lately read of Dr. Johnson applied to another person:—

"In every speech persuasive wisdom flowed,
In every act refulgent virtue glowed;
Suspended factions ceased their rage and strife,
To hear his eloquence and praise his life."

And there was the silent eloquence of a good life in Joseph Sturge; a silent eloquence by which he persuaded men to follow his example, and by which he always fortified and strengthened every good cause to which he devoted himself, and I know of none in which he was not a labourer. A sound judgment, a steady adhesion to his principles when they differed from other men's, a tolerance of which I hardly ever saw the like, perfect charity even towards those with whom he differed most. I need not dwell upon the merits of Thomas Clarkson, the pioneer in the great cause. But I would add that there were pioneers of emancipation as he was the pioneer of abolition, who were not sufficiently before the world because they were not parliamentary advocates of the cause. I name first and foremost, James Stephen. Having been in the West Indies for many years of his life, a lawyer by profession, he was the strong, steady, and inflexible advocate of the slave. He it was who dragged that system and its abuses to light by a constant undeviating course of advocacy out of Parliament, and I look upon him to stand in the same relation towards emancipation as Thomas Clarkson did towards the abolition. I may mention also Zachary Macaulay, who, having been Governor of Sierra Leone, and having actually undertaken a slave voyage, in order to make himself better acquainted in practice with the horrors of the middle passage, devoted himself constantly afterwards to the same abolition and emancipation—and no one after Mr. Stephen served that great cause more. It would be superfluous to mention others, such as Buxton, whose great and ultimately triumphant exertions you are acquainted with, and, though he happily lived to see his work completed, he is one of those whose loss we have to deplore. There are many others whom now to enumerate it is unnecessary; but on an occasion like the present we do an act of gratitude and expediency also, as well as discharge a debt of strict justice, when we recite the circumstances of those who have gone before us. Among others, it is impossible to forget Henry Thornton, the constant coadjutor of Wilberforce in Parliament. And let it never be forgotten that after Fox had been through life a steady advocate of the abolition of the slave-trade—he never lived to touch the question of emancipation—it was by his colleagues, Grey, Lansdowne, and the rest of his Government, that the first Emancipation Act was passed in 1817. To be sure, it was inefficacious, but that was no fault of theirs, for it accomplished all that had at that time been proposed. It dealt with the question by penalties, and everybody knows that the profits of that infernal traffic were so great that a man might safely risk the loss of five or six vessels by seizure, provided he escaped with the seventh vessel. Finding that it was absolutely necessary that we should, for the first time, call the thing by its right name, and that we should no longer slander trade by calling that a trade which was a crime, we treated it as it deserved—as an offence; and I had great satisfaction in prevailing on Parliament to pass a Bill for making the slave-trade a felony, which—so great was the revolution that had taken place in people's sentiments—went through both Houses of Parliament without encountering one dissentient voice. That ended our share in the slave-trade. With the exception of some few capitalists employing their money in that traffic, it has now ceased to be a British offence, and is confined to those foreign nations to whom I have already referred. Now, that emancipation has put the negro on the same footing as the white in point of rights and privileges, it is fit that we should for a moment stop to consider what his behaviour has been under the change; and nothing can be more satisfactory than all accounts of the conduct of the slaves. It was expected by some that, on the 1st of August, 1834, there would be an outbreak, and that the sudden liberation of persons who had so long been confined, and under the influence of oppression, would occasion conduct that was not consistent with the public peace. Never was any apprehension more completely falsified by the result. On that day there was all over the West Indies, I venture to say, among the 850,000 negroes whom we had liberated, the most perfect peace, uninterrupted by riot or debauchery. In that country where nature provokes the passions, and where the stimulus of intemperance is dealt out with a profuse hand, there was no instance to be found in all the Caribbean Sea of intoxication or of riot from intoxication. On the contrary, the churches and chapels were filled. Successions of congregations, one after another, frequented them in order to testify their gratitude to God for the great boon which Providence had bestowed on them. Those people, as pious as the nature of man will allow, spent that day in piety and devotion, and not the slightest breach of the peace or act of intemperance was perceived. Then it was said, "They will not work." The result has proved the contrary. They are not at all indisposed to work. Give them wages and they will work. No doubt they will prefer cultivating their own yam-gardens if you do not give them adequate wages; but, when they have adequate wages, they will work as well as can be desired, not only at cotton and indigo, but at sugar also. It was said at the time that the supply of sugar would greatly fall off; but we have positive proof from the most undoubted authority, that where they are well treated and proper wages are given, the supply of sugar in the district is not diminished by emancipation. Indeed, it was stated by the Marquis of Sligo, some years ago in the House of Lords, that there was one district in his government, he having been governor of Jamaica, in which a twofold greater produce of sugar had been made by free negroes than by slaves in former times. That, I admit, appears to have been a peculiar case, and therefore I do not mention it as an average; but, as a general rule, I say that there has been no diminution in the growth of sugar, and no want whatever of men to work at proper wages. This subject has lately been made a matter of controversy, and an inquiry is now going on from which I hope truth will be obtained, and from which we shall see whether there are not exceptions—as I don't doubt there may be—to that rule. For instance, I am told that Barbadoes stands in a different position from Jamaica in that respect, and that Barbadoes is flourishing. Undoubtedly all the respectable testimony which we have from Barbadoes is to the effect that there is no want of sugar, and that its growth has increased instead of falling off. The former slave stands now in a different position with respect to the community, in consequence of the change that has taken place, from that which he occupied before. He has the same interest now as his master. It becomes his interest that the master should profit, for his wages are to be paid out of the gains of his master. The profits of the planter are the fund out of which his wages must be paid; consequently they have a common interest, and he ought to rejoice in everything that tends reasonably and without abuse to the profit of the planter. That many planters have suffered, that many will continue to suffer, is undeniable; and those particularly will suffer whose estates are under mortgage. It may be said, indeed, that it all depends upon that, and that those whose estates are not under mortgage are flourishing; but as a very great many estates are unfortunately in that condition, I fear that a considerable proportion of proprietors have suffered. But there have been many sufferers also by their advocacy of emancipation, and when I mention the name of Mr. Stephen, I am reminded of the last act of his public life, when, having been the steady supporter of the then government, he, in 1815, gave up his place in Parliament and all hope of preferment, and retired into private life, because he conscientiously differed from his political friends in a question regarding Africa and the slave-trade. Such men also as George Thompson and others, both in this country and the United States, despising the danger to which in some cases they were exposed, and the loss which in all cases they underwent, laboured in this great and good cause, and honour be to their names! I

could name other instances, and, if it were not
selfish and a slight matter compared with the sa-
crifices which others have encountered, I might
name my own case. I grudge not, but look back
with satisfaction and delight to the labour of nearly
sixty years in the cause; but I was about to state a
different kind of sacrifice which I made most cheerfully. I lost an estate in the West Indies which I
should not much have valued, and I lost also an
estate in the North of England which I should very
much have valued, by a kind individual who had
made me his heir to both estates altering his will
because I would not, in 1833, abandon the cause of
emancipation. I only hope that those who follow
us may live to see the last remains of slavery itself
abolished, and previous to that the last remains of
the slave-trade. One has grown old in these labours,
and this is an occasion on which I might say:—

> " E'en in our ashes,
> Live their wonted fires."

It is difficult to avoid the old feeling, which has not
been interrupted, but only relaxed of late years
because the occasion has ceased.

Governor HINCKS, of Barbadoes, moved—"That
on the twenty-fifth anniversary of the abolition of
slavery in the British colonies, this meeting joyfully
records its satisfaction in the retrospect of that great
act of national justice and sound policy, and em-

phatically affirms that the emancipated population of those colonies have triumphantly vindicated their right to freedom, and the justice of the Act of Emancipation, by the signal progress they have since made, morally, religiously, and politically; and this meeting is of opinion that the great event now commemorated, and its results, should animate the hopes, and encourage the efforts of the friends of freedom throughout the world, who are invited to mingle their congratulations with ours, that from the list of human inconsistencies and crimes has been obliterated for ever that of British colonial slavery." Before speaking to the resolution, he defended himself against any who might say he ought not to be present at such a meeting. He would not have been there to engage in anything of a party nature, but the question of slavery was not a party question in this country. And he believed also that the planters were themselves convinced of the good results of emancipation. He had not arrived at the convictions he entertained from his experience in Barbadoes only, but had carefully examined the subject in the Southern States of America, in Cuba, and in the other colonies of the West Indies. The result of his inquiries he had embodied in a letter to Mr. Lewis Tappan, of New York, and, having fortified his opinion since, was prepared to stand by everything he had said.

There could be no doubt in the minds of any who examined the subject, that slave labour was much dearer than free labour. It only required that England should prove this to be so in all the West India Islands, to make emancipationists of the Southern States of America. Hitherto we had not performed our duty to the West Indies, nor to the principle of freedom. The good results of emancipation on the social condition of the people, it was not denied by anybody in the West Indies, had been very great. In Barbadoes the progress was especially marked. He knew of no people anywhere, of the labouring class, who had done so much as the people of Barbadoes had done for the education of their children, and the results were seen to be of the most gratifying character in the social habits and mental acquirements of the people. The Governor quoted a number of statistics to prove this, and then proceeded to remark upon the vicious tenure of land, which was the real cause of much of the want of material prosperity complained of. It was only a monthly tenure, and the tenant was frequently compelled to leave his growing crops, and take for them the valuation of the proprietor; and if he gave notice to leave, he sacrificed his crops altogether. If he were the proprietor of a sugar estate, the first thing he would do would be to set apart the third of that land, of which he would give them as good a tenure as he had himself, if they desired to settle upon it. He would encourage them to grow canes upon the estate. That common-sense view of the case had not been taken. Their plan should be to induce the people, on their own account, to attend to the cultivation of sugar.

Mr. George Thompson rose amid loud applause, which having subsided, he said it would be a work of supererogation on his part to add a single syllable in addition to the very luminous speech just concluded by his Excellency the Governor of Barbadoes. He thought the argument on that branch of the question was impregnable, but if it were not so, they were not there to celebrate the triumph of any dogma of political economy so much as to congratulate one another—the country, the Queen, and mankind at large—upon the extirpation of one of the most heinous crimes ever perpetrated by man upon his fellow. The question had never been in this country, in the days when public feeling rose so high as to sweep away the dams which previously impeded the progress of the abolitionists, a question simply of labour, or of the material prosperity of the colonies; the sympathies of the friends of the slaves were not confined within the circumference of a sugar hogshead; it was not so much a question of giving free labour to the planter, as of giving freedom to the slave. The argument drawn from political economy had been settled long, long before. Adam Smith, Say, and a host of others, had demonstrated that with reference to sugar growing, as to every other human occupation, free labour was better than forced, and human nature and experience alike taught that kind treatment and equitable remuneration were better than coercion and the lash. But even should our political economy be false—should the plantations of the West Indies fall into decay; even should planters and managers have to leave their properties, and seek in other regions profitable occupation, the principle on which the anti-slavery cause was based would stand unshaken, for that principle was that emancipation from bondage was the right of the slave, and that his enslavement was a crime to be abolished, not an evil to be mitigated, or an institution to be perpetuated for the profit and aggrandisement of a particular class. He (Mr. Thompson) thought it well, on an occasion like the present, to glance backward to the period when was manifested the germ, or first principle, of that movement which, in twenty-two years afterwards, was consummated in the abolition of the slave-trade, and in five-and-twenty years from that epoch, was succeeded by the abolition of slavery. Mysterious, indeed, were the ways of Providence! In that year a humane man—the Vice-Chancellor of the University of Cambridge—announced a prize for the best Latin essay on the question, " Is it right to make slaves of others against their will?" A young man, then a student in one of the colleges, entered into the competition. He construed the words of the thesis into a reference to the African slave-trade, and resolved to prepare his essay accordingly. He was wholly ignorant on the subject, and had but a few weeks for the accomplishment of his task. He gained access to the manuscripts of a deceased slave-trader, and held conversations with some officers who had been in the West Indies. By accident he saw an advertisement of Anthony Benezet's *Historical Account of Guinea*, and hastened to London to buy it. The contents were all he wanted, and he sat down to his work. That work he had entered upon as a contest for academical distinction, but he soon found it changed into a painful investigation into the character and details of an inhuman system, the curse of the world, and the scandal of his country. As he proceeded, his imagination was filled with horror, and his heart melted with pity; sleep fled from his eyes and tranquillity from his soul. He finished his essay, he read it in the Senate, he received the prize, and with his manuscript in his pocket he started for London. Let his own pen describe what took place on the way :—" I became at times seriously affected while upon the road. I stopped my horse occasionally, and dismounted and walked. I frequently tried to persuade myself in these intervals, that the contents of my essay could not be true. The more, however, I reflected upon them, on rather upon the authorities on which they were founded, the more I gave them credit Coming in sight of Wade's Mill, in Hertfordshire, I sat down disconsolate on the turf by the roadside, and held my horse Here a thought came into my mind (oh! what a thought was that in its influence and its consequences), that if the contents of the essay were true, it was time some person should see these calamities to their end. Agitated in this manner, I reached home." The man into whose mind that thought came, was Thomas Clarkson,—and the year was 1785. Mr. Clarkson early secured for the great cause in which he was the pioneer, the inestimable services of Wilberforce, eminent alike as a scholar, an orator, a statesman, and a Christian; and while the philanthropists of England gathered around these champions of the negro's rights, they were not without coadjutors in the two Houses of Parliament Amongst them were many illustrious names:— Viscount Howick (afterwards Earl Grey), Lord Henry Petty (afterwards Marquis of Lansdowne), Lord Grenville, Lord Holland, William Pitt, and Edmund Burke, and then, through successive years, Mr. Wilberforce brought the subject before Parliament, but could not succeed in carrying a bill for the abolition till 1804. The measure, however, was rejected in the Lords, and the following year the Commons threw out the bill. The cause triumphed during the short administration of Mr. Fox, and the Whigs had the honour of abolishing the detestable system. Thus was matured and brought to fruition the wayside thought of Thomas Clarkson. A society for mitigating and gradually abolishing slavery was afterwards formed, but its efforts were unattended by any practical results. At length occurred the case of the missionary Smith, which was taken up by the noble chairman in the House of Commons, and occasioned one of the most remarkable debates on record. The speeches of the noble lord were amongst the greatest ever delivered in the British Senate; for forensic skill, for impassioned eloquence, and for oratorical splendour they were unsurpassed. The noble lord had said truly, that the discusion of that question did more than anything that preceded it to bring about the freedom of the negro. The noble lord met with a suitable reward; for the generous effort then made, and for his speech in 1830, he was elected as the representative of the most important constituency in England—he was returned member for the county of York, and successor of the parliamentary champion of the negro's cause, William Wilberforce. About this time the Anti-Slavery Society made an important alteration both in its principle of action and its mode of operation. It inscribed upon its banner, "Immediate, not gradual emancipation," and it sent forth men to summon, by the living voice, the people to a grand and final struggle. The Reform Bill passed, and a Reform Parliament was convoked. Everywhere candidates were pledged to immediate abolition. The result was, that in the year 1833, the Government had a House prepared to pass their measure for the extinction of slavery. When the fate of the system was sealed, there were those who cherished painful apprehensions respecting the conduct of the negroes when they should learn the tidings, and when they should become free. Mr. Buxton, from his seat in Parliament, addressed to the slave population the counsel of a Christian statesman, and urged upon them the forgiveness of past injuries, and the observance of a strictly quiet and orderly demeanour. [The speaker read the passage from the printed debates.] This, said the speaker, was counsel worthy of a Christian statesman. Was it given in vain? Did the negroes, to whom it was offered in strains so touching, accept and act upon it? Did they justify either the honest apprehensions of their timid friends or the affected fears of the interested alarmists who sought to scare the nation from its duty? Or did they rather excel the advice given them, and by the unexampled character of their deportment far exceed the wildest hopes which the most confident among their benevolent and trusting sureties had ventured to cherish? History answers the question. Her scroll extends over twenty-five years. She has recorded the events of the 1st of August, 1834, when, according to the title of the Act, slavery was abolished throughout the British colonies. History has also recorded the events of the 1st of August, 1838, when the unjust, unnecessary, and cruel system of apprenticeship, was prematurely brought to an end.

Lord BROUGHAM: I omitted to notice in my remarks the fact that the 1st of August is also the anniversary of the accession of the House of Brunswick to the throne of these realms, by which we were saved from religious thraldom and arbitrary power.

Mr. THOMPSON: I am grateful for the interruption, for the coincidence is a most interesting one. Respecting the emancipation of the negroes, I may say, without risk of contradiction, that the annals of our race would be searched in vain for a parallel instance of a transition so sudden and complete from slavery to freedom, so undisfigured by any abuse of the power which liberty bestows. What are they now? They are free men, exercising the liberty, the rights, the privileges, and the power of free men. Have they abused their liberty to the destruction or injury of their former oppressors? Have they relapsed into barbarism and the usual vices and slothfulness of barbarians? Have they slighted or misused their opportunities for the advancement of their material, moral, intellectual, or spiritual improvement? I point to the facts for an answer. They are industrious cultivators, and often the independent freeholders, of the soil. They are the liberal promoters of education. They are devout members of Christian churches. They sustain out of their own resources the worship of God, and the various religious institutions of their own locality, and even send to the treasuries of societies in this country their liberal contributions. There is no department of agricultural, commercial, mechanical, or political life, into which they have not entered, and in which they have not creditably distinguished themselves. After dwelling upon other topics, and enumerating the many eminent persons who had laboured in the cause of the African race, Mr. Thompson concluded as follows: The immortality of this unsurpassed galaxy of the great and the good is assured. When the infernal slave-trade throughout the world is utterly exterminated, when the last fetter of the enslaved negro is rusting away, when Africa is restored to peace and blest with civilization and Christianity, then will these names be household words amongst millions of that race with whose redemption they are imperishably associated—and then, also, will be remembered another name—a name linked for more than half a century with the cause of freedom and progress in this country—a name indentified with education, with the freedom of the press, with the reform of the law, with the advancement of science, with the liberation of commerce, and with the amelioration of the social condition of the masses of our people—a name which has become a synonyme for whatever is brilliant in oratory, or nervous in diction, or powerful in invective, but a name illustrious for this reason chiefly, that amongst those who during that period laboured most, and most successfully, to secure for the negro the rights of humanity, and the immunities of a citizen, the foremost in the battle, as the latest survivor in the victory, was Henry Brougham.

Mr. Thompson sat down amidst loud and repeated cheers.

A Spanish gentleman, who gave the name of MORENTIN, a teacher of languages, rose and asked leave to address the meeting on the subject of the first resolution. He wished, as a Spaniard, to state that his countrymen, who felt strongly upon the subject of political liberty, sympathised, he was certain, with the society on the subject of emancipation.

The CHAIRMAN said he was sure the meeting

would be gratified by the communication which the learned professor had made.

The Rev. W. G. BARRETT, who had been for several years a missionary in British Guiana, said that on Aug. 1, 1834, he commenced a succession of services, and from six o'clock in the morning till six in the evening, without any intermission, he was engaged in speaking to this emancipated people. When the negroes in the West Indies received this great boon, they were willing to bury all the injuries of the past, and to unite in singing with one heart, as they did with one voice, " Let us sing unto the Lord, for he has done great things for us, whereof we are glad." Had the conduct of the planters been as forbearing as that of the slaves was forgiving, and their administration as wise as the cause of the negro was just, there would have been none of those heartburnings of which they were perpetually reading, both in the Colonial and in the English press. Mr. Barrett then read an extract from a speech of Count Montalembert in the French Chamber of Peers bearing on the abolition of slavery in the West Indies. The passage, which throughout was very eloquent and striking, concluded by characterizing the abolition of slavery in the British possessions as " the most delightful spectacle and the most blessed revolution which the nineteenth century had presented to man." He would say one word with respect to British Guiana. In British Guiana the emancipated slaves had become larger occupiers of land than those of any other colony. There were, by both canals and along the banks of the Essequibo, large estates which had been abandoned in consequence of the inability of their proprietors to pay for labour. The negroes had, in many cases, united in numbers of, in some instances, one hundred or two hundred, and put their money together to buy these estates. Some of these estates were seven, eight, nine, or even ten thousand acres in extent. They had got them under cultivation, occasionally employing the same white manager to conduct it, under whom they had toiled in bondage. He (Mr. Barrett) was in British Guiana several years, and never received a farthing from any missionary society whatever. He was the minister of a large congregation entirely of negroes. His wife was the only white woman among them, yet they supported him comfortably, and when she was ill they, without any solicitation at all, raised a sum of money, in order to enable him to make a tour for the benefit of her health. He was happy, he said, to throw in this humble contribution to the great cause of humanity and freedom.

The resolution was then read, and carried unanimously.

The Hon. AMASA WALKER, formerly Secretary

of State for Massachusetts, moved the following resolution :—" That while this meeting deeply deplores the fact that slavery is still maintained by various civilised nations, and that the slave-trade, with all its horrors, is still prosecuted in contravention of treaties, and in defiance of all attempts for its suppression, it rejoices that in different parts of Europe, and in the United States of America, there are societies zealously engaged in promoting the extinction of these iniquities, and would cordially wish them ' God speed.' " He felt, he said, great pleasure in uniting with England in the commemoration of a day which had emancipated 800,000 human beings—a day which had reflected high honour upon England and which was a cause of rejoicing to all mankind. He rejoiced to have such an opportunity, on behalf of three millions and a half of his fellow-creatures, to return his sincere thanks to the chairman, and all who took an interest in the cause of emancipation. Ever since he could remember, the name of Lord Brougham had been associated with the cause of freedom. They would ask him what was the prospect of emancipation in the United States? It would be deeply gratifying to him if he could tell them that the day was dawning; that they hoped soon to have another August 1 to celebrate.

Lord BROUGHAM : It should be the 4th of July.

Mr. WALKER: They also had thought that that should be the day. He was sorry to say he could give no such account. He would not, from pride of country, come there to present anything in a false light. To one question, what is the prospect of emancipation? he must say there was none. Why? Because cotton was 14 cents a pound. (Laughter.) They would give that for it, and so would all the markets of the world. The consequence was this, it had the protection, in such a price, of being 150 per cent. higher in proportion to the labour it cost than other agricultural productions. The demand for slave labour was increased, the price of slaves rose, and the prospect of emancipation declined. It rose and fell with the price current. As long ago as 1852, the Legislature of Virginia came within a very few votes of abolishing slavery. Why? Because they were at very low prices. They might depend upon it that 14 cents a pound was a very powerful lens, and planters had looked through it till they saw that slavery was the corner-stone of republicanism, and they had even discovered that it was a divine institution. Planters looking through it, had made out that the slave-trade was the noblest missionary enterprise in the world. The American and the English were one family, having a common origin, speaking a common language, and, thanks be to God, having a common destiny too. Slavery could not be crushed out in England and sustained in America, but the abolitionists of both countries must stand shoulder to shoulder in the great contest for freedom.

Lord BROUGHAM rose and stated that he was obliged to return to the House of Lords. The last speaker, he said, had alluded to the opinion held among the pro-slavery party in America, as to the antiquity of the institution; but he (Lord Brougham) knew of one far older, not much worse, and very much connected with slavery. It was murder; for the first man that was born into the world murdered the second. He would only address them in the words used by a great Roman orator to a great Roman soldier:—" Depend upon it your fortune has nothing more propitious than that it gives you the power, and your nature has nothing more excellent than to give you the will, to promote the security and the happiness of millions."

The noble lord then left the hall, the whole assembly standing up and cheering warmly.

Dr. HODGKIN then took the chair, and presided over the concluding business of the meeting.

Mr. WASHINGTON WILKS seconded the resolution. He said he was anxious that this celebration of a great epoch in the history of Britain and of mankind should not simply minister to our national pride, but should also stimulate us to the discharge of present duty. It was, unhappily, necessary, in the first place, to maintain what had been achieved and to prevent the revival, under whatever flag or whatever disguise, of the atrocious traffic in human beings. But slavery was a perpetuation, a daily repetition, of the horrors of the slave trade—and slavery was, as they had heard, a material institution in a country not less English than their own. They must not rest while the tongue of Shakespeare and Milton contained the word "slave" as descriptive of a still existing fact. It would be a shame if this English celebration passed off without a word of honour to the names, and encouragement to the labours of those noble men and women—the abolitionists of America. Garrison and his associates had been stigmatised as un-Christian, but he ventured to say, as there was no denial of Christ like that of holding in bondage those He had died to free, so there could be no faith more orthodox, no lives more holy, than those of the martyr spirits who held nothing dear to them so that they might preach the gospel of negro liberation.

The resolution was unanimously adopted.

Mr. STEPHEN BOURNE, of Jamaica, proposed, and the Rev. W. H. BANNER seconded, a vote of thanks to the chairman, and the proceedings terminated.

The Conclusion.

Little chinks
Let in great light.

ET us rejoice that such men as Wilberforce and his compeers have been raised up to be blessings to their fellow-men; that while others have been the begetters of war, and all that can degrade the human character, these men have been given for our "betterment;" they have been as lights set upon beacons, guiding that portion of the human family—that most oppressed and cruelly tortured of it—the negro of Africa, to find peace, and to stand by his white brother A MAN. Let us thank the "Giver of all good" for these great blessings, and cherish within our breasts hallowed thoughts for our national and universal benefactors, and pray that God will inspire the hearts and strengthen the will of other nations to imitate our example,—to set the negro free; not only set him free, but show him that he is a responsible creature, whether in work (for he is not an idle being, as some would make us believe, but as honest and upright as the white, if only properly treated, and guided with a little of that discretion which we are wont to give to the training of the nonrational portion of God's creatures) or in the social and.civil circle in which he moves.

Could nations only, without prejudice, use their pen and paper in a little simple arithmetical exercise, they would soon demonstrate that slavery, wherever and in whatever condition it is found, is a losing game—losing to the national honour of any nation who encourages it. I believe that if the Americans could be once thoroughly convinced that slavery is a losing game, the question would soon be settled. Show them, and it is possible to do so, for the fact is all that goes to make up prosperity in a nation lies in singular *excess* on the *free* side. Show them the number of acres under cultivation, the amount of produce, the difference in the value of land, the number of miles of railroads, the number of banks, of schools, colleges, and other places of instruction, and the worshippers of the Great Dollar who, in that cause, are the most earnest men in the world, will soon become fanatics even in the cause of Freedom; for such data are the most powerful arguments of the whole, and are sure to find converts and disciples, and none more easily convinced than brother Jonathan.

It is nonsense to talk of abolitionists wishing to ignore the rights of others—of the adverse party—that the slave-owners have as much right to their view of the side of the argument there can be no doubt—the erring side ought to be heard—but let any unprejudiced man say whether they have produced satisfactorily, the least satisfactory grounds for holding a right in the free made man. They, the pro-slavery men, say there are tremendous interests bound up in the subject; there are appalling difficulties, social and commercial arguments in extenuation of the " Institution," all of which is granted, but the thief finding himself in the hands of *justice* might plead the same *appalling* difficulties, &c., arguments as foolish as they are unjust.

That a crash will come sooner or later, in which slavery shall sink below the contending waves, and freedom arise on the shores of the United States, no one can doubt, but it must be a work of time; wild schemes of a day will not annihilate the cancer of centuries. It is very humiliating, but quite true, that often justice has to be shelved for the sake of expediency—and I believe, that long, long ago, the United States would have been freed from the blot, had not expediency, brought about in a great measure by such wild schemes, made it appear to the upholders of the "Institution" as dangerous to their safety. However, had Jefferson's proposal been adopted, this evil would have vanished. Unfortunately, evil counsels prevailed; and the children are suffering for the sins of their forefathers. The incubus, I say, might have been got rid of with safety, dignity, and wisdom. What has been the result? Wild schemes have been propounded, and wilder plans attempted, the whole question has become embittered, and a life-and-death feud has sprung up where the sole chance lay in friendly and unimpassioned relations; steady-going minds have flung themselves with heat and ardour into the fray; gentlemen have become ruffians while discussing the best mode of dealing with the curse, and are now occupied in shedding each other's blood; Christians have developed into heathen ferocity; and even the best wishers to the cause of freedom have retired from the scene. The result is, that Abolition in the United States has been delayed yet another generation, to the grief of all honest men, and the confusion of all wise ones.

This is viewing slavery as a £ s. d. matter — a matter of commercial interest, and which must ultimately give way. If viewed through a Christian's telescope, the aspect is very different—there no half-measures are seen in the background, all is as clear as the beams of heaven's light can make it—the men whom the Almighty has made of one blood, we must view as brethren, and through good report and evil report we must ask all mankind to recognise *all* as such. Dr. Cheever, of the United States, a gentleman whom every Christian, whatever be his peculiar tenets, must heartily wish God speed in the efforts to arouse the attention to the enervating, corrupting, and desolating influences of slavery in the United States—one who has seen with his own eyes, and therefore speaks from experience, must command respect, and more than ordinary attention. He says, speaking at a late meeting of the Friends of Freedom:—

"I am so unaccustomed, in the conflict against the great iniquity of slavery, to the language of sympathy and kindness, encouragement and applause, that I hardly know how to acknowledge the very great and delightful heartiness of my friendly reception here on this occasion. To the friends of the enslaved is given the great privilege of suffering for Christ's sake, and, up to the very eve of the abolition of slavery, that, perhaps, will be the result of earnest and persistent labour in this cause.

"The life and forces of a country are expressed in two directions—its religion and its laws. A mere evil may be borne in patient resignation, or left to time and gradualism for its amelioration. But when not merely a burden but a sin is laid upon men's shoulders, and bound there by the religion and the laws, then and there, coeval with such a wrong, there arises an obligation of incessant protest, disobedience, and moral resistance; and, if this resisting dictate of conscience and of God is not obeyed, every man becomes a voluntary party to the guilt, complicated personally in it, and accountable for it. Those are bound to resist first and strongest who are nearest to God, most completely and clearly in His light—that is, His church, His people, armed with His Word, commissioned from Him with His Spirit and truth. If the servants of God, who, really fearing Him, as Burke said, fear nothing else, would just take this work and pursue it, there would soon be a settlement on right grounds, and no iniquity could stand before a people armed with God's righteousness and trusting in Him. Our great work now in America is to rouse the Church and ministry, armed with the thunderings and lightnings of God's Word, against this complicated and infinite wickedness of slavery. You can have no adequate conception of its devastating, uncontrollable sway. It has taken captive the greatest minds, suborned the most enlightened consciences, commanded the services and debauched the principles of the most acute and colossal legal intellects, and retained in its behalf the greatest masters of a gorgeous and imaginative rhetoric. It has set the

seal of a complicit, guilty silence upon the most
orthodox pulpits and the saintliest tongues, with as
undisputed and submissive a resignation as ever
followed the touch of heaven's fire upon Isaiah's
mouth for his celestial eloquence. It has opened
consecrated lips to forswear and forbid in the very
sanctuary even the privilege of prayer for the
enslaved, as endangering the stability of the Union
by the possibility of an answer. Its empire over
men's minds is complicated out of every element of
influence, and secured by every security of selfishness
—complicated as a vast network of law, monopoly,
prejudice, power, pride, interest, fashion, social
habitude, perverted Scripture, false and inveterate
opinion, licentiousness, truth held in unrighteousness, and the unrighteousness ecclesiastically ad·
mitted and enforced as the interpretation of the
truth; all these snares thrown upon society, and,
as the result of the complicity of the Church, a
conscience seared as with a hot iron—a judicial
blindness, the being given over to strong delusion
to believe a lie.

"There is no possibility of exaggerating the
terribleness of the congeries of cruel opinions, propositions, arguments, and laws concentrated in this
system, of the hideousness and execrable impiety of
which, examined by the Gospel, but especially when
considered as having been contrived and established

under its light, no symbol can convey any adequate conception. The slave code of the United States is a knotted pyramid, as of skulls and serpents, of cruelties cabled into law, reminding us of the sight that once in a South American wilderness nearly froze Humboldt's soul with horror—the spectacle of a pyramidal column of living congregated snakes, interfolding, interknotted, in one body, but with heads and necks shooting forth in individual snaky vitality from the corporate solidity and socialism. The slave system being the governing system and power, and the Constitution itself being interpreted according to its requisitions, the jurisprudence of that system is the ruling national jurisprudence; and the consequence results that, by reason of the multiplied and vast related interests, the prevailing sentiment and sensibility becomes a habit of cruelty and oppression, and an absolute jealousy against equity, as being the enemy of the vested rights in this system of iniquity.

"To this dreadful pass we have arrived. I think you never came to this, either in the growth of your colonial slavery, or in your moral, spiritual, and parliamentary conflict against it. Dreadful as that system was, you little know the power and horror of it at your own doors,—a pestiferous, social, and religious tyranny of cunning and power, setting its seals on every habitation, its minister and altar of moral death and worship in every household. You never arrived at the deliberate wickedness, in your national jurisprudence, of declaring that black men have no rights that white men are bound to respect, and that precedents of antique mischief and darkness are to be set as the rule of Christian practice and law, so that, whenever your judges find in past centuries of ignorance and insensibility any inhuman, barbarous, detestable opinion prevalent, sanctioning any atrocious cruelty, they are bound to enthrone that in the place of justice, and, instead of rectifying a past error and abolishing a past crime by the light of Christianity and the decisions of equity, they are bound to seize and impress Christianity and equity itself as legal servants of the crime and forerunners of the wickedness. The mark of American justice on the whole coloured race is that of vagabonds upon their native soil and of criminals, that every one that findeth them may slay them. When Cain was sent forth from Eden, though red with the blood of his brother's murder, the mercy of God provided for him against the vengeance of private retribution; but American slavery, and American justice at the bidding of slavery, brands not only its immediate victims, but their whole affiliated race in colour or in blood, as the legitimate prey of every social pirate, and pursues them everywhere with implacable ferocity, denying even to injured in-

nocence a pity that the very justice of God accords
even to crime.   You never had a whole tribe of
judges legally commissioned, and new tribunals
established, to see to the complete and perfect execution of cruelty and crime against a whole race of
millions of innocent beings. You never had the
Constitution of your country perverted, scandalized,
and made a tool of tyranny and cruelty, by a forgery
foisted into it, a series of diabolic cyphers frau-
dulently inserted at the right side of the figure 1,
and thus making the unit of freedom and justice, a
million of iniquity and slavery. The dead flies of
your ointment you take out as fast as the nostrils of
the people perceive their offensive savour; our slave
moralists and legislatures carefully preserve them,
and grind them up, and distil their essential oil to
penetrate the whole mass, as the very essence of its
preciousness and fragrance. Bad as some of your
judges at one time were, you never had even one
Jeffreys so inhuman as some of the creatures of
slave law; and, above all, your laws were never yet
constructed on the principle, and your judges chosen,
disciplined, and rewarded by the same rule of
favouring wrong instead of right, and pressing the
utmost exactness of cruel law against mercy, against
liberty, and in behalf of cruelty and slavery. But
the nature of our system of slavery, and of the laws
contrived to uphold it, of which the infamous

Fugitive Slave Law is an example, is such, North as well as South, that it may be said of those judicially ordained to these functions, as it was at the vilest period of Judean wickedness, her judges are ravening wolves; and we have had cases of men sending helpless babes, whose mothers have fled with them into a free State, back into the hell of slavery, under pretence of service due, as if there could be such a thing as service due from a babe whose only faculty is that of tugging at its mother's breast—service due from the babe to the pretended owner of the mother, or the possibility of such service—so that a literal impossibility is made the ground of a pretended contract; and on the figment of such contract is grounded the claim of perpetual property, descending, as an entailed inheritance of course, from father to son, on the part of the pretended owner, and of cruelty and misery on the part of the innocent victim of such iniquity, to the latest generation. We have had such cases, and worse than such, in which the only suitable figure emblematic of such justice, and of such monsters as such justice educates, would be not merely the ravening wolf, as drawn by the pen of Divine Inspiration, but the statue of a hyena of the desert with an infant child upon its tusks.

"Now, I may safely say that you in this country never have had such a colossal work to accomplish

as the destruction of such a system as this, right at
your own doors; your own merchants imagining
that the stability of your wealth, and even your very
existence as a nation, were bound up in its per-
manence; your own neighbours, and those that go
with you to church, and the church that admits you
to her communion, and the ministers of God that
break to you the bread of life, upholding and
justifying the whole iniquity, infected with it, under
subjection to it. You have not had to endure an
enforced silence of your pulpits, on pain of being
deprived of your chosen spiritual guides; and your
pastors have not been under the temptation of
keeping silence at the peril of distraction and
divisions in their churches, banishment from their
parishes, and almost starvation. I know that your
faithful non-conformists laid the foundation and
fought the battles of your own religious freedom at
just such cost, but you never have had this conflict
unto death against slavery. Yet the peril is no just
excuse for silence or inaction. I am reminded of a
good Quaker's reply in our country to a pro-slavery
minister, who told him, when he had been inquiring
why he did not take the ground against slavery,
‘Why, Sir, you know we are dependent on the
people for our bread, and we must live.’ ‘I see very
plainly the fact of your dependence,’ was the answer,
‘but I do not see so plainly the necessity or im-

portance of your living.' Here, at home, at least
from the time of Lord Mansfield's decision, and
through the influence of some of your noblest
statesmen and divines, and, with some exceptions,
throughout the whole body of your literature, your
moral philosophy, your poetry, and the principles of
your jurisprudence, from Bracton and Coke down-
wards, you have had a tide of power to drive against
this iniquity, and it has been to you a foreign evil
and sin. At length, by the grace of God, you have,
at a great cost, broken the chains from 800,000
slaves in your Colonies. God has, by training you
to this magnificent act, put you under bonds for the
emancipation of every slave on the face of the whole
earth, and has given you the means of fulfilling this
obligation. He has given you an authority and
power towards us greater than that of all your
navies; nobler, grander, mightier than that of all
your armies; more legitimate, more irresistible. He
has prepared you to be what we cannot yet be,
because our hands are red with African blood—
God's priesthood to a world. Be ye clean, ye that
bear the vessels of the Lord. In whatsoever vice
God commissions us to attack, we can do nothing if
we leave it in the power of the enemy to say,
Physician, heal thyself! The spread-eagleism of our
Fourth of July eloquence is all hypocrisy and
fustian, when, at the very same moment that we

mounted to the clouds, as on eagles' wings, the vulture of slavery, with the crooked talons of our slave laws, is perched upon our national tribunal of justice. Now, by the grace of God, you are free from this iniquity, however in time past it must be said, And such were some of you; and by very virtue of your having been yourselves conspicuous in this guilt, and renounced it, and, to the praise of God's grace be it spoken, renounced it through the conviction of its wickedness, you may be to the rest of the world a royal priesthood, to show forth the praises of him who hath called you out of this darkness into his marvellous light.

" It is a literal impossibility for me at this time to intimate, even in general, what I would be glad to spread before you in detail. But I may say two things, induced especially by recent development and pressures. First, you may help us greatly by grappling with the dreadful prejudice against colour, and rebuking and denouncing it. Treat it, as well as the slave-holding which is at the bottom of it, as a wickedness expressly forbidden by the Almighty. It is the spawn almost solely of Southern slavery, and we have had in our own country recently a demonstration of the infinite hypocrisy of this prejudice, which has not even the merit of being natural, is the sheer creation of circumstance, in the procession through our cities of some sixty

or seventy Japanese, with a skin as tawny as
that of our mulattoes; and if they had been dressed
in a slave's trousers, with unshaven crowns, they
would any of them, perambulating the Southern
States, have been clapped up as good slave material,
thrown into prison as vagabonds, and sold to pay
their gaol fees. But their colour has not prevented
their being followed and flattered, caressed and
fêted, as no retinue of strangers ever has been
since Lafayette visited our country. Such a demonstration of the falsehood of the existence of
any natural prejudice against colour as an instinct is
almost ludicrous. The truth is, if the Africans could
be placed at the top of society and the whites at
the bottom for one or two generations, the prejudice
in regard to colour would unquestionably be
reversed also. Let the wealth and power of
society be placed at disposal of the coloured race,
and the sentiments and the very theories of men
would change in favour of their sootiness.

"The examples and the efforts of Lord Brougham
against the workings of this wicked prejudice are
admirable. He has brought to the notice of Parliament, the recent outrage committed against a
respectable American family, on board one of the
Cunard steamers, for the alleged crime of African
blood in their veins. Now we honestly think you
may properly judge this, on board a British

steamer, to have been a worse outrage than the expulsion of a coloured person would be, from the cars on an American railroad. When Mr. Dallas refuses a passport to a native American because of the darkness of his skin, he commits an insult against God and humanity, which is perfectly natural in the official of a great slave power; but it is unnatural and doubly criminal in a servant of the British people and Government, to take part in such insults. It is to be hoped that the people of Great Britain will not wink at the manifestation of such an inhuman and insulting prejudice, nor suffer its continuance under the British flag, in a corporation wholly and proudly British, but, in this instance, most basely subservient to the slave power. If they legitimatise and sanction such outrages, it need not be surprising that in America the people go further, and protect the slave-trade itself under the American flag. Considering the immensely overbalancing amount of base and selfish interest for the support of the system in America, it would be no more than fair to make this concession. If you admit an ounce of cringing to the slave power, and of deference to its insolent dictates here, you must expect at least a pound there. I speak this to your glory, that you are now on such a height in regard to this iniquity, that a degree of complicity with it which would be regarded but as a very small matter in America, becomes here a great sin. It would be almost as bad, and quite as mean, in your Cunard steamers, if they should be found admitting the slave power to regulate the social code upon the sea, in deference to this villany, as it is in New York merchants to turn pirates for the profit of the villany itself. Your public press, whenever it apologises for slavery, is incomparably baser than ours in New York, even in their open advocacy of the crime. And we do think that a pro-slavery man or machine, be it in the shape of preacher, editor, or press, in such a country as yours, that will burn incense before this Dagon, that will volunteer in defence of any part of this worship, that will so needlessly insult and slander the anti-slavery sentiment and reputation so justly yours, is a manifestation of baseness that ought to be quite impossible. It might be pardoned comparatively in the United States, where, as Burke once said in better times, something must be pardoned to the spirit of liberty; so now you might almost say something must be pardoned because of the despotic infection with the spirit of slavery; but here in England there ought to be no pardon, no endurance of such a monstrosity, nor anything but condemna-tion and contempt for the writer, orator, or corporation, infected by such a spirit. If men live in a land of the malaria of fever and ague, it must be expected that nine-tenths of the inhabitants will have 'the shakes,' especially if they are taught to believe, by the physicians of the country, and the ministers of the Gospel, that 'the shakes' are an essential element of health, piety, and long life. But for men in a healthy country, and under a sound and not insane dispensation of the Gospel, to inoculate themselves with the disease, and go about in ague fits, and strive to communicate it to their neighbours, that they may make more money out of cotton and quinine; for men to adopt a foreign idol, the sin of another country, purely from commercial and political considerations, to fall down before the imported image of an outworn and execrable barbarism merely for the profit of such idolatry, this surely would be a more desperate debasement of conscience, a worse renouncement of God, and of all that is noble in humanity, than the continual worship of one's accustomed native idols. I have only to add, on this point, that, if in this country and the United States the churches will resolutely adopt and apply the principles which your admirable Bishop Wilson has adopted and applied for the extirpation of the evil of caste in British India, the prejudice will be conquered and destroyed.

" I may say, in the second place, that, having been yourselves redeemed from this iniquity by God's mercy and grace, and clearly now seeing and knowing its sinfulness, you may do much for our deliverance by religiously and conscientiously treating it as a sin, necessarily excluding those that practise it from membership in the Christian Church, and to be rebuked in those who sanction it as directly and inflexibly as the sin of idolatry, or adultery, or murder. You would not endure among you in Christian fellowship those professed Christians who would sanction these crimes, even though themselves not personally defiled with them. You would not endure a defence of the morality of the brotherhood of Thugs or Mormons. Let us, therefore, mark with as stern and pungent a condemnation those who defend and receive as Christians the brotherhood of slave-holders. There is great gain in calling sins by their right names, especially if God Himself has defined and characterised them. Jonathan Edwards—whose sermon against the slave-trade and slavery as being a sin as inherently sinful as murder, preached in 1791, is as perfect a specimen of what is now denounced as fanaticism as you can find in the English language down to this date of 1860—says that the Africans being by nature equally entitled to freedom as we are, and having the same right to their freedom which they have their property or their lives, to enslave them, or to hold them as slaves, is as really, and in the same sense, wrong as to murder them. He applies the same

inexorable logic, taught by the Word of God, to
every case, and declares that ' it is as really wicked
to rob a man of his liberty as to rob him of his life.'
To hold a slave he declares to be this crime. And
he demands to know how it is possible that our
fathers and men now alive, universally reputed
pious, should hold negro slaves, and yet be the
subjects of real piety, since to hold a man as a slave
is a greater sin in the sight of God than concubinage
or fornication. He addresses himself to slave-
holders, and says to them, ' You daily violate the
plain rights of mankind, and that in a higher degree
than if you committed theft and robbery.' In this
tremendous sermon he does not extend his view to
the infinite exasperations of the crime to be found
in the entailment of its guilt and misery from
generation to generation, by slave-breeding and
child-stealing for missionary purposes; the conception of such supra-Satanic hypocrisy and
wickedness never entered into his comprehensive
mind. Nay, he expected the speedy abolition
of the whole iniquity, and declared that the
light against it was so increasing that he would
venture to predict that within fifty years from
that time it would be as shameful for a man
to hold a negro slave as to be guilty of common
robbery or theft. Seventy years have passed away,
and if the author of this sermon were permitted to

come down from heaven, walk through the Southern States, behold four million human beings bought, held, sold as merchandise, enter the city of New-haven, walk across the green and shady park of the churches and the colleges, and find that by the leading pastor among those churches the highest possible sanction of slave-holding is maintained in the defence of the American Board of Commissioners for Foreign Missions, in their admission of slave-holders into their missionary churches, and that, by his avowal, the rejection of a slave-holder from communion in the Christian Church was an almost universally repudiated principle of church discipline, and that now not the sin of slavery was denounced from the Word of God, but the uncharitableness, the malignity, the madness of those who affirm slavery to be essentially and inevitably sinful; the discovery that such a Christianity as he believed on earth had ripened in the second generation unto such fruits, would be almost enough to carry him back into heaven an infidel.

"And here it is that we must take our stand, and direct the truth, as the truth is in Jesus, upon the central citadel of this infernal abomination, and shoot the excommunicating lightnings of God's Word against it. For maintaining this position, which is the only position and claim that can be maintained consistently with the Word of God and the purity of the churches, the few who have thus far insisted upon it in the United States have been attacked, abused, and slandered.

"No longer ago than last October it was my privilege to propose a sweeping resolution at the annual meeting of the New York State Congregational Association, and after an earnest discussion, notwithstanding the opposition of some of the leading members of the body, it was carried with a slight alteration—'Resolved, that the holding of slaves is in all cases an immorality, the renunciation of which ought to be made a condition of membership in the Christian Church, and that the sin of slave-holding is one against which the law of God and the Gospel ought to be proclaimed in preaching persistently until this iniquity be overthrown.' This was a victory of righteousness. But in the same month a resolution of a similar character, offered at the meeting of the American Board in Philadelphia, and intended to apply to the missionary churches, was rejected utterly, and I believe unanimously. And to illustate the disastrous influence of such a refusal by the Board to treat slave-holding as a sin, I may mention the fact, that when, at one of the Choctaw missionary stations, a convert who was a slave-holder, and had been received as such into the church, called upon the missionary to tell him that he felt distressed in his conscience as to the incon-

sistency between holding slaves and belonging to
the church, that missionary immediately handed to
the conscience-stricken convert a tract entitled, 'An
Argument for the Divine Right of Slavery.' It was
a religious tract, such as the American Tract Society
might have issued in perfect accordance with its
pro-slavery policy.

"Whatever thy hand findeth to do, do it with all
thy might. We are not to regard ceremonies, rules,
conventionalities, nor to give the enemy any advantage by admitting for one moment the claim of
any vested rights in wickedness. We must cut
through every entanglement of sophistry, every
Gordian knot that cannot be untied, every consideration of a sacred expediency, and we must enter
boldly into the sanctuary, and take the divinest
shewbread from the altar, if it be necessary to save
life. We must despise and trample upon the insolent
fastidiousness that proclaims the Sabbath and the
pulpit too holy for such themes. The slave-holder
will hunt his slaves with horses and hounds upon
the Sabbath-day; indeed, it is his favourite season
for such ferocious sport. And which of these most
orthodox observers, so jealous for the honour of
God and the sacredness of His Sabbath that they
denounce you as madmen, and desecrating, blas-
phemous, and political pulpit ranters, if you presume
to advocate in God's name, and on the Sabbath-day,

the claims of oppressed and bleeding humanity in the person of the slave, if they had an ox or an ass that should fall into a pit on the Sabbath-day, would not lay hold on it and lift it out? We will be instant, in season and out of season, in scorn and defiance of such infinite hypocrisy. We will take a lesson even from negro sagacity and energy. During the war of our Revolution, in one of its darkest periods, and at one of its most perilous posts, Washington found that night after night the sentries stationed at a very critical point were picked off in some unaccountable, undiscoverable way. At length he called to him a very trusty negro in the army, in whose presence of mind and courage he had great confidence—a *negro citizen*, in spite of justice Taney's infamous decision—a negro citizen to whom George Washington would have given a passport, signed by his own hand, of protection as an American citizen all over the world, and to this man Washington committed for that night the watch at that point of danger. He impressed upon him his directions as to vigilance, and the manner of the watchword, which was, to call out, if he heard any movement, 'Who goes there?' three times, and then fire. The faithful, keen-witted negro received his commander's instructions, revolved them in his thoughts, and made up his mind accordingly, determined to keep them even to the letter. Past midnight, when all was silent as the grave, he heard a suspicious, stealthy step advancing, and discerning a shadowy form through the darkness, he levelled his gun, called out with a rapid voice, 'Who goes dere tree time?' and then instantly fired. The foe was killed, the plot discovered, and the position saved. It is just thus that, by rapidity and boldness, by admitting nothing, by taking advantage of every technicality on the side of freedom, by pressing to the uttermost, in letter and in spirit, every claim of righteousness and justice, we mean to outwit and overcome our infernal adversary, for we are not ignorant of his devices.

"In this conflict, Great Britain must assist us in the uncompromising application of the Word of God. There are two phrases that have done good service from two great masters in your country, the one of fervid and practical piety, the other of philosophy, law, and practical statesmanship—phrases that have cut as with the sweep of a two-edged sword—the one phrase from John Wesley, as to the practical diabolism of the system of slavery, that it is 'the sum of all villanies;' and the other from Lord Brougham, reprobating 'the wild and guilty phantasy that man can hold property in man.' This latter is the grand principle which we find in the Mosaic statutes—principle on which the man that holds a fellow-being as a slave, the man that makes merchandise of man—which it is impossible to be a slave-holder without doing—is reprobated of God as a man-stealer, and, along with the murderer, is condemned to death. This impossibility of a righteous property in man, this righteous and inexorable treatment of slavery, according to the dictates of natural and revealed religion, is the destruction of the system."

The following enumeration of the Slave States of America will be read with painful interest, being now the only civilized part of the world in which slavery is recognized as a legitimate institution:—

In 1796, when Washington ascended the presidential chair, the slave states were Virginia, Maryland, North Carolina, South Carolina, Kentucky, and Georgia. The small slave state of Delaware was next added. In the same year the state of Kentucky was formed out of territory lying within the ancient limits of Virginia. The importance of multiplying the slave states, in order to give the slaveholders a preponderance of power in the government, was soon felt by them. Every new one gave them two additional senators in the upper chamber, having the power of voting the appointment of the government, and upon all bills, excepting upon those relating to money. In 1789 the state of Tennessee was formed out of territory in North Carolina, and thus an eighth slave state was added to the Union.

In 1802 Alabama and Mississippi, both formed out of territory in Georgia, became the ninth and tenth slave states. In 1803 the all but illimitable territory of Louisiana was ceded by France to the United States by purchase, it having been previously wrested by France from Spain without consideration. For that territory, stretching from the Gulf of Mexico to the Rocky Mountains, France received 15,000,000 dollars. Out of that territory three states were formed—Louisiana proper, Arkansas, and Missouri. In 1821 a new slave state was formed through the purchase of the Peninsula of Florida, with the Gulf of Mexico on the one side and the Atlantic on the other. For the last thirty or forty years the avowed intention of the slave-holders had been to annex the whole continent of America, south and south-west first, and afterwards to seize on the island of Cuba, then the Antilles, and in fact never to stop in their career of chattel despotism until they had subdued the whole of that vast continent to the dominion of slavery. Florida, which was obtained by cession from Spain, made the fourteenth slave state—one more in number than the whole of the states together at the time of the Union. Then came one of the most piratical wars ever beheld on the face of the earth, when the slave-holders crossed the Sabine, and penetrated into Mexico, where slavery had been abolished by a decree of the Mexican republic. There the Americans took their slaves. At first they humbly sued for protection, and got it from the Mexican government; and then, when strong enough, they turned round upon their benefactors, and wrested from them a territory almost as large as France; and the almost limitless territory now termed New Mexico was extorted by the American government as some compensation for the trouble and expense of the war. The area at present occupied by the slave power was double that of the whole territory of the United States at the time of the Union. There were but thirteen colonies at the time they declared themselves independent of Great Britain. The produce of the slave states in the single article of cotton had advanced from three bales in 1789 to 4,500,000 in 1860, of which England bought for her manufactures as much as cost her £35,000,000. In the single article of cotton alone, irrespective of her other commercial transactions, Great Britain has done more to perpetuate this abomination, than the rest of the civilized world altogether. Not wilfully, I think, but simply from exigent circumstances, which will be removed as new fields open in our own colonies for cultivating cotton. I feel satisfied that there is not a cotton-buyer in this country but would gladly give up purchasing slave-grown cotton if he could.

Look at Slavery in whatever light we may, it has always the shame of the country upholding it; it bears the stamp of wrong both on the obverse and the reverse: wrong not merely in the abstract, as is often admitted by its apologists, but wrong in the concrete also, and possesses no one single element of right. Look at it in the light of principles, and it is nothing less than a huge insurrection against the eternal law of God, involving in its pretensions the denial of all human rights, and also the denial of that Divine Law in which God himself is manifested. Founded in violence, sustained only by violence, such a wrong must by a sure law blast the master as well as the slave; blast the Government which does not forbid the outrage. Moreover slavery must and does breed barbarians. It is barbarous in its origin; in its laws; in its pretensions; in the instruments it employs; in consequences, in spirit, and wherever it shows itself.

Before we close this chapter it may be worth while to ask, what has this country done to bring about the annihilation of the traffic in slaves by other nations? Since 1815 we have expended upon an average more than forty million pounds sterling, *i. e.*, we have devoted to that special object more than one million pounds annually. These figures must show that Great Britain is not merely a talker but an earnest doer in trying to put a stop to the horrid traffic. And I think nothing so much shows the hold that this abominable and inhuman trade has upon the interest of the traffickers than the fact that all this money has been spent to no purpose, or at least to no permanent good; and I believe that if £40,000,000 were expended every year, the good effected would not be one jot more satisfactory; simply because the Spanish Government will not prohibit the importation of slaves into Cuba. If Spain would, or could be induced to, discontinue the traffic, not only the slave-trade, but our enormously heavy expenditure would be at once ended. She owes us something like £400,000; for that sum she actually received to discontinue the traffic. I say she *owes* that sum, inasmuch as she has broken faith with the country in receiving the money and not adhering to the letter of the agreement, viz., the cessation of the slave-trade. In China, if a poor Celestial does not keep faith with us, we are not long before we teach him that we will not be trifled with. Why should the Spanish government fare better, or be more tenderly dealt with? And that there is now, more than ever, a reason for striking a blow, we have only to re-echo the voice of the *Times*. It quotes :—" A commodore on the African station writes to the Admiralty that the slave-trade 'is now [1860] conducted on a scale fully as formidable as it was ten years back.' A rear-admiral reports that

' for many years back the prospect of putting down the slave-trade has seldom been less encouraging.' " Then again the British Commissary Judge at Havannah, in a communication to the government at home, refers to the " enormous increase of the slave-trade within the year" [1858].—Lord Malmesbury writes to the British minister at Madrid, that the slave-trade is undoubtedly carried on in Cuba " to an extent little, if at all, inferior" to that which prevailed before its abolition was agreed upon ; and, finally, Lord John Russell gives us the latest statistics on the subject, by declaring from his place in the Commons, this very session, that from thirty to forty thousand slaves are imported into Cuba every year from the coast of Africa, in despite of all our endeavours to intercept the supply, by that which is (pacifically viewing the matter) our only mode, viz., our eternal and expensive blockade. Add to this the loss of thousands of lives, as well as that of numerous costly vessels of war and the aggravated character of sufferings endured by the poor sailing slaves, no unprejudiced man will hesitate for a moment as to what ought to be done. Stop it by fair means if possible ; and if not, by severity. The winking at it is a disgrace to us—to us holding and professing the doctrines of Christianity. I will only state two more facts, and leave every Christian reader to ask his own heart to declare what ought to be done. Out of every one hundred negroes captured on the coast of Africa, sixty-six are *sold* in Cuba. A negro on the coast of Africa is bought for £4, and he is sold in Cuba for TWO HUNDRED POUNDS!!!

But let us change the scene to one more pleasing :—

It is really most extraordinary how great events seem to revolve in periodical parallels. Fifty years ago, our legislators were just about to give to their West Indian slave colonies the first foretaste of freedom; and, at the very time that the Birthday of Freedom was being celebrated in London in 1859, we heard that the serfdom in Russia, which is only a very slight remove from absolute slavery, was receiving its first blow—a blow which, let it be hoped, will be followed by others, and which shall cause the death of the tyrant (Slavery) there with as satisfactory results as the death blows did to his power in *our* negro West Indian colonies twenty-five years ago. The present Emperor is a man of enlightened views, touched also with the feelings of humanity; and no sooner was he relieved from a demoralizing war, than he turned his attention to the serf question. "Active, intelligent, and kind-hearted, Alexander II. saw and felt how necessary it was to relieve his empire from the stigma of slavery, and how much more powerful he would become as the ruler of 60,000,000 freemen." It appears from the journal that "In the course of twelve or fifteen years, serfdom shall be entirely abolished, and the serf shall be a freeman; that the house in which he has been living, and a small portion of land, shall be his property, or that of a free community, whereof he is a member." Many valuable concessions have been added within the past year, to these humane intentions, by the noble Emperor of Russia. This is only the beginning. God and England approve your noble and generous intentions, *Great* Alexander II. of Russia. And that his good example may be followed by all the world,—

> "We pray
> That all mankind may make one brotherhood
> And love and serve each other; that all wars
> And feuds die out of nations, whether those
> Whom the sun's hot light darkens, or ourselves
> Whom he treats fairly, or the northern tribes
> Whom ceaseless snows and starry winters blanch.
> Savage or civilized, let every race,
> Red, black, or white, olive or tawny skinned,
> Settle in peace, and swell the gathering hosts
> Of the great PRINCE OF PEACE. Then all shall be
> One land, one home, one faith, one friend, one law,
> Its ruler God, its practice Righteousness,
> Its spirit Love!"

THE END.

"What thoughts crowd through the memory as we ponder on a hundred years ago. A hundred years ago, when William Wilberforce was born to fulfil the mission on which he had been sent, and to give freedom to millions. A century after that notable birth, and five-and-twenty years after the fulfilment of that mission, we have a tribute published to the memory of the liberator. We need not say a word to recommend to our readers the little book; *every Englishman will wish to possess a memento.*"—*The Standard.*

"It is enlivening to read of the efforts, and remarkable success which attended them on the part of this champion of the slave. We commend the volume to the attention of our young friends, believing they will be interested by its contents."—*British Friend.*

"This little book, which is very prettily got up, is a rapid, enthusiastic, and somewhat discursive review of the life of Wilberforce. It is thickly interspersed with appropriate reflections. We shall be glad to learn that it has had a large and remunerative circulation."—*Anti-Slavery Advocate.*

"A MEMORIAL of the "Slaves' Champion" cannot fail to prove interesting to all who value the blessing of personal liberty. His warm advocacy and increasing exertions in order to accomplish negro emancipation, give to the name of WILBERFORCE a title to occupy a prominent place in the annals of the British Empire. The volume lying before us contains matter quite sufficient to exemplify the life and times of that Christian philanthropist, or, as Lord Brougham termed him, "The venerable patriarch of the cause of slaves." He was the man who in this instance virtually gave to man his birthright—freedom to the slave! The writer is well known as the author of 'The Popular Harmony of the Bible.' &c., &c. We can speak in favourable terms of this work, as inculcating sound Christian principles; it 'is also well written, and interspersed with interesting remarks on many eminent men, who were Mr. Wilberforce's cotemporaries."—*The Christian Examiner*

———

N.B.—The Author's Address is at the end of the Advertisements.

"An admirable guide to the study of Holy Scripture. * * The teacher, no less than the student, will find it a great acquisition."—*John Bull*.

"An important aid in the process of imparting Biblical knowledge. It embodies the best information on the subject to which it relates."—*Evangelical Magazine*.

"A most valuable aid to the profitable reading of the Scriptures. * * It appears to us as complete in detail as it is admirable in arrangement, and useful in aim."—*Christian Times*.

"It is by far the most practical and useful publication on the subject extant. Alike in phrase, form, and matter, it is what it professes to be, popular—a book for all Scripture readers."—*British Banner*.

"A book for everybody who reveres the study of the Word of God. It is a compendium or digest of all that has hitherto existed, and is incomparably the best thing of the sort we are able to name."—*Christian Witness*.

———

Hebrew for Self-Instruction.

Price 3s. 8d., post free.

Has been highly spoken of by the Press, several Journals having set up Hebrew type to illustrate their critiques.

Address—H. M. WHEELER, Author of "Slaves' Champion," &c. Hammersmith, W.

When the price of the foregoing works is sent in Postage Stamps, THREE additional stamps must be included for exchange.

Post Office Orders, on Hammersmith, payable to HENRY M. WHEELER.

THE AMAZING GRACE OF FREEDOM

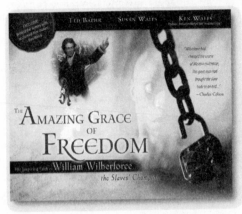

THE INSPIRING FAITH OF WILLIAM WILBERFORCE, THE SLAVES' CHAMPION

COMPILED BY

TED BAEHR, SUSAN WALES, AND KEN WALES

The year 2007 is the landmark 200th anniversary for the Slavery Trade Act, legislation that led to the eventual abolition of slavery in Britain. Spearheaded by the legendary man of faith, William Wilberforce, the legislation marked a victory in the 30-year personal effort to see the brutal captivity and trade of human beings come to an end.

- An exciting "sneak peek" behind the scenes of *Amazing Grace* with photos and exclusive interview with producer Ken Wales on his six-year journey of faith to see the movie come to life

- Extraordinary presentation, focused on Wilberforce and his example of how God can use one person of faith to change the world

- Featuring select essays and commentary from top scholars and ministry leaders: John Piper, Chuck Colson, Alveda King, Herbert Schlossberg, D. James Kennedy, and more!

- Historic paintings, engravings, documents, and unique illustrations are highlighted on every page in the gorgeous four-color interior

CASEBOUND • 10 X 8 • 144 PAGES • $19.99
ISBN 10: 0-89221-673-5 — ISBN 13: 978-0-89221-673-4

Available at Christian Bookstores Nationwide

WILBERFORCE: AN ACTIVITY BOOK

PAPER • 8½ x 11 • 32 PAGES • $6.99

ISBN 10: 0-89221-672-7
ISBN 13: 978-0-89221-672-7

24 READY TO USE LESSON PLANS
BY ANDREW EDWARDS AND FLEUR THORNTON

- Fun and educational lessons for elementary students grades 3-5
- A great companion to *A Journey Through the Life of William Wilberforce*, using fun activities to reinforce historical facts.

This educational and fun activity book and guide for elementary age students is a great start for younger children wanting to learn about the fascinating abolitionist William Wilberforce. A great resource for homes and schools alike, this 32-page, fact-filled book features word searches, fact boxes, and so much more. A great way to introduce elementary age students to a man who changed his world and ours. It's "edutainment" of the highest quality.

A JOURNEY THROUGH THE LIFE OF WILLIAM WILBERFORCE

FOUR COLOR • 5 x 8 • 128 PAGES • $13.99

ISBN 10: 0-89221-671-9
ISBN 13: 978-0-89221-671-0

- Comprehensive hisorical overview — perfect for students ages 12 and up
- "....These pages are intended to commend something of that life to the reader and to convey the enduring truth that we ourselves can live our lives in service to God and in service to others." - *from the Preface by Kevin Belmonte, consultant on the movie,* Amazing Grace

Walk the fascinating pathways and historic halls of England as you retrace the steps of legendary abolitionist and staunch Christian man of faith William Wilberforce. This full-color, unique guide to Wilberforce's life was written by Kevin Belmonte, one of the world's leading scholars dedicated to educating the public about William Wilberforce. It includes descriptions of Wilberforce's work on behalf of social issues, portraits of him and his contemporaries, and photographs of historical sites in England. An excellent educational tool to bring history to life.

Available at Christian Bookstores Nationwide